P9-CFP-095

PENGUIN

ARKANA

CROSSING THE THRESHOLD

The ancient science of astrology, founded on the correlation between celestial movements and terrestrial events, recognizes the universe as an indivisible whole in which all parts are interconnected. Mirroring this perception of the unity of life, modern physics has revealed the web of relationship underlying everything in existence. Despite the inevitable backlash as old paradigms expire, we are now entering an age where scientific explanations and models of the cosmos are in accord with basic astrological principles and beliefs. In such a climate, astrology is poised to emerge again as a serious study offering a greater understanding of our true nature. Arkana's *Contemporary Astrology Series* offers, in readable books written by experts, the insight and practical wisdom the world is now ready to receive from the newest vanguard of astrological thought.

Linda Reid, QA (FAA), has been a full-time astrologer since 1978 and established the Matrix School of Astrology in Tasmania in 1988, with a correspondence division in 1990 to service students in distant country locations. Born on 12 March 1940 at 1.27 a.m. GMW in Leeds, England, she began investigating the dynamics of the unconscious during a five-year stay in Ghana, where she was privileged to study local jujumen and their shamanistic cultural practices. While living in South Africa, she was introduced to astrology and began a lasting love affair with the cosmos. Moving to Tasmania in 1972, the study of dreams and, later, their interface with astrology, began in earnest. She is married with two daughters and specializes in psychosynthesis and dreamwork as a support system to general astrological counselling. Experience has proved that using the astrology of dreaming is a profound way to make the motivations of the unconscious manifest in conscious life and many valuable life changes have occurred as a result of listening to and acting on the messages of dreams.

CONTEMPORARY ASTROLOGY
Series Editor: Erin Sullivan

CROSSING THE THRESHOLD

The Astrology of Dreaming

LINDA REID

ARKANA
PENGUIN BOOKS

ARKANA

Published by the Penguin Group
Penguin Books Ltd, 27 Wrights Lane, London w8 5tz, England
Penguin Books USA Inc., 375 Hudson Street, New York, New York 10014, USA
Penguin Books Australia Ltd, Ringwood, Victoria, Australia
Penguin Books Canada Ltd, 10 Alcorn Avenue, Toronto, Ontario, Canada m4v 3b2
Penguin Books (NZ) Ltd, 182 – 190 Wairau Road, Auckland 10, New Zealand

Penguin Books Ltd, Registered Offices: Harmondsworth, Middlesex, England

First published 1997
1 3 5 7 9 10 8 6 4 2

Copyright © Linda Reid, 1997
All rights reserved

The moral right of the author has been asserted

Set in 9.5/12 pt Monotype Garamond
Typeset by Rowland Phototypesetting Ltd, Bury St Edmunds, Suffolk
Printed in England by Clays Ltd, St Ives plc

Except in the United States of America, this book is sold subject
to the condition that it shall not, by way of trade or otherwise, be lent,
re-sold, hired out, or otherwise circulated without the publisher's
prior consent in any form of binding or cover other than that in
which it is published and without a similar condition including this
condition being imposed on the subsequent purchaser

TO MY DAUGHTERS
Amy Elise and Charmaine Felicity
embodying earth and water, fire and air

Contents

List of Illustrations

Acknowledgements

I want to acknowledge first and foremost my husband Bob for the love, support, patience and tolerance he has shown over the past thirty-six years when I have been 'off on another planet'. I especially want to thank Dennis Georgakis, friend and guide, for his gentle criticism, sensitivity and clarification in helping me sort out my argument from my passive voice during writing and his helpful advice and great sandwiches! Special thanks to my friend and associate Lyn Dickson, for great synastry, 'being there' and acting as a sounding-board on the occasions when my Aries Moon got the better of me, as well as for her most valued insights into the human condition. Thanks are due to Carol Gray, the epitome of Moon conjunct Neptune for the stream of dreams, love, trust and loyalty across the 'generation gap'. Carol is living proof of the grace of soul. Lynda Hill brings symbol to life and I would like to thank her for her reassuring and joyous faith in living; her faxes and calls appear just when I need them despite her frenetic schedule. Sylke Rees, thank you for your humour and honesty, for being the only person who would dare to tell me when I am over-reacting, and for the subtle links of understanding that are between Pisceans. Erin Sullivan saw the possibilities when the book was just an idea and gave me the necessary infusion of determination and discipline to follow through as Saturn transited my Sun and I almost receded into the infantile bliss of my fourth house. I first mooted the idea to Erin as Pluto entered Sagittarius and formed a trine aspect to my natal Pluto at the Revisioning Astrology Conference in Melbourne in 1995. It was indeed a meeting that catalysed profound change. Christine Stribley supplies me with healing energy and unconditional friendship and long astrological discourses and is a lifeline at times when I just need talk. Christine Broadbent and Stephen Hill at Planet Camp in New Zealand provided a retreat and healing at a time of despair, turning negative into positive and are the embodiment of what elegant astrology is about. Thank you to all my students, who have put up with distraction and delays, and from whom I learn so much, and to David Targett, for firing the arrow that started the journey. All charts and grids in this book have been produced using 'Solar Fire', supplied by courtesy of Stephanie Johnson and Graham Dawson.

Introduction

He who would interpret a dream must himself be, so to speak, on a level with the dream, for in no single thing can one ever hope to see beyond what one is oneself.

Dr C. G. Jung

One autumn day many years ago I was renovating an old garden. After a few hours of raking leaves and pruning hedges I sat for a few minutes to rest under a lovely tree and closed my eyes against the sunlight. What evolved from that moment was to be the catalyst for opening a whole new dimension in my astrology as a beautiful coppery creature began to climb down from the tree and slide effortlessly to the ground. In semi-human form, naked and gender free, the figure was covered in soft downy hair, shining, silky and tactile. He, for I call him 'He' without knowing who 'He' is, took my hand gently and led me to a fallen log, where we sat comfortably together for a few minutes, contemplative, sharing a smoke from a clay pipe that 'He' produced from nowhere.

After a little while my companion again took my hand and led me on a tour around my own garden. He showed me gilded turtles under fallen fences and bronze spiders with topaz eyes. Silver snakes emerged from debris and slid over my feet on their way to meet lizards of the most exquisite colours. Gentle rabbits and baby creatures of a kind I have never seen shared the garden with porcupines whose spines were tipped with silver. Luminous flowers grew in places I didn't know and dissolved at my touch or wrapped stamens gently round my fingers, and butterflies of all hues emerged from crannies and feasted on their nectar. We entered a flower and marvelled at the stamens, perfect in their spiralling formation, following the path they made as if in a forest of strange trees. This tour of a familiar landscape now filled with unfamiliar sights seemed to last for ever until, to my regret, my guide placed a few small acorns into my hand, made a gesture of farewell and ascended the tree again. I tried to call him back and only realized that I gave voice when a call from the house asked why I was calling.

Only then did it filter through to my conscious mind that indeed I had experienced a separate reality, the entry to which was most natural and undefined. For some minutes I was bemused, unsure of what was real and what was surreal; glancing at the sky, I noted that both the late afternoon sun and the pale rising moon were visible in the heavens. I felt that strange feeling, a portent we tend to call intuition, but was unable to identify its cause. I 'knew' that something had happened at an inner level but couldn't define it. I felt I had learned something of value, that my dream guide had shown me something that had to have import in my conscious life. I knew that the appearance of the Sun and Moon simultaneously were making a statement that constellated in this knowledge, whatever it might be. Unfortunately, I was not yet aware of the value of charting the dream so I have no chart of this moment in my life.

Some days later a client phoned me and told me of a dream she had experienced. She gave me the time when she awoke, as she wondered 'if the time had any significance'. The synchronicity of these events were to lead to research and development of methods of using dream charts in better understanding of my work. It is the fruit of that research that is presented in this book, in the hope that other astrologers and dreamworkers may gain additional tools to support their clients, as well as grow in understanding through their own dreams.

It is not my intention to give arbitrary interpretation of symbols as they appear in dreams – the reason will become clear in reading the book – but to give instruction on how to set about using dreams and their timing to integrate astrology and its symbolic roots with the manifestations of dreams. For this reason, some of the astrology may seem fundamental to the practised astrologer, but it is my hope that it will add another 'tool' to their astrological practice; that it may be instructive to the student of astrology and encourage them into a deeper study of symbol; and that it may encourage those in other disciplines to consider the phenomena of time and space in their clients' lives.

For if a man should dream of heaven and, on waking, find within his hand a flower as token that he had really been there – what then, what then? Thomas Wolfe

I

Mapping the Dream Landscape

Almost suspended, we are laid asleep
In body, and become a living soul:
While with an eye made quiet by the power
Of Harmony, and the deep power of joy
We see into the life of things.
William Wordsworth

Dreaming as a phenomenon is possibly the most fascinating aspect of psychic life that we experience. Even those who claim to dream rarely will, at some time, dream a dream that has an impact on their lives. As a species, we have a natural and instinctive curiosity about the workings of our inner life – we seek to rationalize and understand what our dreams are telling us. In interpreting dreams we tend to seek to understand the imagery as though it were external to the self, a set of moving pictures with ourselves as observer. This is in some ways correct – the dream does indeed present a pictorial and symbolic drama, but the images are not external, they are the creations of our own unconscious minds, generated by the unconscious, brought into consciousness where they become specific, a part of the process that Jungians call 'individuation'.

At its most simplistic, individuation is the constant and instinctual urge to complete ourselves, to experience a sense of wholeness. Being whole means to reconcile that which we innately sense as divided or separated: to reconcile those opposites we have come to understand as the conscious and unconscious components of the self. Wholeness of self must embrace both the conscious and the unconscious, the rational and the irrational, the objective and the subjective, the profane and the sacred, the worldly and the etheric, as paradoxical components of the divided self.

The first step to individuation is the recognition or awareness of the separation within ourselves. We can gain such awareness through dreaming.

Individuation is a continual interchange, a relationship of antitheses, as the psyche attempts to reconcile the division. When dreaming, we leave behind the solid ground of conscious reality and enter another reality, just as solid and meaningful. While we are dreaming, all figures, activities and symbols seem natural and real. Only with a return to consciousness do we question and attempt to gain knowledge from what has taken place in the landscape of dreams and in doing so we tend to intellectualize dream images, again separating the two mirrored realms of our being.

I believe the unconscious mind has intuitive understanding of the cyclic nature and pattern of the universe deeply rooted in the collective unconscious, and so can select an opportune time to create a dream with specific meaning to enable us to return to consciousness with insight. Each dream has a purpose, a context. The realms of consciousness and unconsciousness are not rigid or non-interactive; they are not static but fluid, evolving and in constant interchange. Even on waking, seemingly aware, we are in a state of '*circumambulation*', a Jungian term that implies a cycle or spiral of involution and evolution. The whole self is in a state of flux, around the centre of self – the personal 'axis'.

There is an interchange between inner and outer – the experiences of waking life are drawn into the unconscious and the unconscious contents of the mind brought to consciousness, in a series of convolutions. The contents of the unconscious are fully available during waking hours, if we are alert to them. Experiences in conscious life are drawn into the unconscious, towards the centre, where they are transformed and returned to consciousness. The transformation occurs without our knowledge, except when we wake to remember a dream. We then get a brief glimpse into the transformation process in action. We 'see' our own evolution.

Working with dreams gives the opportunity to see at first hand the reflective nature of our day-to-day lives, but will not provide the complete answer to every problem. The mind creates its own metaphors and none so obviously as those in the dream drama. The simplified interpretation of symbols depends on a too-literal and external viewpoint, which denies the dreamer the healing and understanding that comes through subjective exploration. So, while we seek rational understanding of dreams, it is equally valuable simply to accept that, in dreaming, some compensatory healing occurs. Dreaming is essential to our well-being and may indeed contain a 'message' of reconciliation that can be explored and developed towards better understanding of our whole lives. We must feel our dreams as well as attempt to intellectualize them.

Our mental powers, in the unconscious reaches of the mind, function imaginatively in expressing the soul's intent. That these expressions may seem distorted only intrigues and provokes us into a deeper search for meaning. These mental powers also function as recorders of the universal truths imprinted on the psyche – not the deceptions and half-truths told to ourselves at the conscious level. They use our facility for memory to bring dream images into consciousness so that we can see the truth. Mind, then, is central to the psychic process of individuation.

For ancient cultures, sleep was a dark time when the human soul left the body to explore the collective realms of the unconscious or mystical. The belief that the human soul reconnects with the universal soul in sleep, and that whatever is experienced in sleep through dreams is an actual experience of the personal soul, is a belief that can hold true even in today's societies. Sleep has long been employed as a healing therapy. In the temples erected in honour of the mythic healer Asklepios the ancient Greeks practised the ritual invocation of dreams for healing purposes. Typically psychic disturbances were the cause of ancient ills just as they are the cause of modern-day malady. Hypnotherapy, active imagining and the reworking of mental dilemmas and attitudes are all ways in which we seek to achieve psychic health and, as a consequence, conscious happiness, well-being and empowerment. In all of these practices we use the power of the mind, suggestion and the contents of the personal unconscious through dreaming.

Perhaps the ancients were more aware than we are today that physical illness reflects psychic ill-ease and that the healing power is within the psyche along with the dis-ease. The infirm, both spiritually and physically, were brought to sacred sites, wrapped in bandages of cowhide and treated with herbs, so that, in an incubatory sleep, they might be visited by the healer god Asklepios, whose spirit entered the soul of the dreamer to promote healing. Being like a newborn baby equates to entering, in humility, into sacred space, the landscape of soul, childlike and vulnerable. It is only in that state of acceptance that the wisdom and healing powers of the unconscious are available to the whole self. The word Asklepios may have an ancient Semitic root meaning prostration, a ritual act of abandonment to the powers of the gods. The dream experience itself is therapeutic, and the practices at the ancient Asklepion temples illustrate the healing capacity of dreaming beyond rational explanation.

The psyche has its own in-built Asklepion in the unconscious, and we reach it through our dreams. In connecting to the source of personal and collective healing, we access the healing energies of all individuals. Since the beginning of time people have dreamed. Their imagery and symbols have become part of the collective pool of knowledge, love and healing, in what has come to be called the collective unconscious. Spiritual healing as a practice is undertaken by many who are aware of their ability to give healing energies to the collective pool and to draw from it at a personal level. Many individuals and spiritually based groups can identify the power of these collective 'temples' of inner healing. The healer god Asklepios personifies the capacity we all have to heal ourselves psychologically. By dreaming we gain access to the collective unconscious; we connect with the universal source of healing, bringing that healing into our consciousness; by adopting a respectful attitude to dreaming and by developing an understanding of the unconscious, we connect ourselves in a brotherhood and sisterhood with others of our species. We are able to add love and healing to the collective pool in an exchange that, ideally, will benefit humankind and help to heal the psychic malaise of the species. We do this by affirmation, in our daily lives, and can do so by affirmation as we sleep. A prayerful attitude to dreaming is essential to contact the healing energies – and by prayerful I mean that we need to take seriously and approach with reverence all that is revealed in dreaming.

So the healer Asklepios can be seen as the symbolic personification of our own capacity to self-heal. The work of Asklepios is essentially connected with soul and dreaming. In dreaming one is restored and transformed and all who venture into the underworld, in dreams, in meditations and in therapy, return in some way healed and whole; dreaming is not 'just one of those things' that happen to us, it is the life-force of the soul.

The dream is the natural process of maintaining a healthy psyche and it is to our advantage to examine the messages of the unconscious. It is essential to appreciate and accept that the healing and reconciliation occurring through dreaming affects our worldly activities. The unconscious, the realm of the soul, continually tries to redress and compensate for the negative experiences of conscious life and, in some dreams, to relive the joy of positive experience, with the firm intent to heal and get our conscious lives into more empathy with the inner-soul journey. Dreams are spontaneous – we cannot make ourselves dream, any more than a 'bad dream' can be discarded simply because we don't like its content. Sometimes it is not necessary to understand the whole meaning of the dream but simply to accept and feel that a change has occurred. In the words of Dr Peter O'Connor, 'Dreaming is the most natural, obvious, and readily accessible means for remembering our imaginal inner world. It balances the proliferation and domination of our existence by our outer reality. Not to listen to and be attentive to dreams is to choose to be psychologically amnesic, at best, and psychologically dead, at worst.'[1]

Dreams often present a confusion of images which, on first analysis, are seemingly unconnected. For simplicity I will call the unconscious part of the psyche 'soul', and I see dreams as essentially the soul's struggle to integrate, meld and blend the internal world with the external, worldly life of the dreamer. Dream images may be reflecting current life situations; they may be harking back to buried experiences and memories, or memories that are part of the human collective. The language of dreams is passionate, moody, eloquent and emotive. It is active, illusionary, allegorical and symbolic, so why seek to assign specific rational interpretations and deductive keywords?

When seeking to understand dream imagery, we should seek not so much to interpret but to comprehend the personal connections. We should do this through amplification and dialogue, and not through arbitrarily assigning a specific standard interpretation to a symbol. Thus to interact with the images and symbols of the dream in a creative way is to strike up a relationship with the images, by exploring their personal connections. This dialogue unfolds the meaning encapsulated in the symbol. Reducing a dream to simple meanings dries out and denies the joy of exploring the unconscious.

The Hindu priest dreams his dreams with symbols that connect him to similar images expressed by the British businessman. The New Guinean tribesman experiences the dream dimension filled with the same symbolic beings as does the Australian stockman. However, we need to make a personal connection with the images, otherwise the commonality with the collective does not exist for us. Our dreaming mental imagery is subjective, yet partakes of the imagery of the collective. The dream reflects the dreamer's inner truth, and the entities of the dream in themselves make no statement unless connected to that truth in a subjective way – while images exist in a collective sense, they must always link to the dreamer's reality, for without personal and individual overtones a symbol is meaningless. It only has existence through the dreamer's personal connection in the unconscious. When an image is brought into consciousness, the significance of the image is qualified by personal expectation. It is impossible to assign an arbitrary meaning to a symbol. We must take into account the subjective value of the symbol, that is the intra-psychic reality of the dreamer.

The dream as a psychic phenomenon offers the most effortless route to the unconscious and carries a tacit as well as an explicit meaning. According to Jung,

The dream is a little hidden door in the innermost and most secret recesses of the psyche, opening into the cosmic night, which was psyche long before there was ego consciousness, and which will remain psyche no matter how far our ego consciousness may extend . . . All consciousness separates; but in dreams we put on the likeness of that more universal, truer, more eternal man dwelling in the darkness of the primordial night. There he is still the whole, and the whole is in him, indistinguishable from nature and bare of all egohood. Out of these all-uniting depths arises the dream, be it never so infantile, never so grotesque, never so immoral.[2]

Indeed, the Greek word, *psyche*, means 'soul'.

Dr Jung did not set up a standard interpretation for images. He viewed dream interpretation as conditional, each symbol an unconscious expression, the meaning of which depends entirely on the context in which it occurs and on the specific conscious and unconscious situation of the dreamer. Effectively, this means that any symbol will have a different meaning according to the context in which it is manifested and so we cannot say that a symbol or image has the same meaning for every dreamer. It is not the intention of this book to interpret specific images in dreams but to give some astrological guidelines for working with dreams: understanding how the images form from the archetypal meaning of planets; using an astrological chart to delineate the potential for healing and reconciliation of problems; and clarifying the intention of the dream, reflected in the timing of the dream and its connection with conscious living. The conditional framework is described by the astrological natal chart and current life situation of the dreamer, and synchronizes with the movement of the planets.

Dialogue with the dreamer and development of the dream imagery is always the most creative approach to dreamwork, but by itself it can be inconclusive. Even given that we understand the value of dreaming as a healing experience, it is in our nature to want to draw a conclusion from the experience. In our search for inner meaning and purpose we do not always come up with answers we would like. The value of the dream chart lies in being able to define that area of conscious experience that might be healed, individuated or resolved as part of becoming whole.

For the professional astrologer, dreamwork, using a chart as a map of the dream, is a way to offer a client support during difficult phases in their lives. Using the dream chart, the astrologer can teach as well as counsel. The astrologer plays an active role in empowering the client to experience and understand the changes that are occurring, not only in their conscious life but in their unconscious life as well. The individual natal, or birth, chart shows the inherent potential for dealing with life and life's dilemmas. With the birth chart, we can determine changes of attitude and direction using the various astrological tools at our disposal, but the insight of dreams gives us an added tool for counselling. In counselling, it opens up a dimension for acceptance of change, for healing and adjusting, as it allows the astrologer to guide the client to an understanding of how dreams are a part of their psychic adjustment in times of change.

We need have no fear of dreaming, even if the images are disconcerting, for all dreams have a purpose. Fearful images of monsters and demons cannot do harm. When we bring them into the light of day their power to invoke terror dissipates, as we realize that they cannot live without our approval. If we are able to isolate the facet of our unconscious lives where our demons lurk, and face what may emerge from the psychic shadow, we can dispatch the demons by looking them in the eye and transforming what may be a negative experience into self-knowledge.

Dreamers often speak of experiencing a 'nightmare'. This is often a misnomer, one we adopt to explain what is an uncomfortable or unacceptable dream experience, filled with imagery that is challenging, feelings that we wish to forget and details we remember with apprehension. The true nightmare is characterized by the fact that only feelings remain; the images fade and are forgotten. On waking, we are confused, and while the dream figures remain momentarily with the dreamer, they quickly fade as full consciousness takes over. The true nightmare is a rare event, and what we are most often dealing with is a 'bad' dream. A bad dream has the same purpose as a 'good' dream, but is simply more graphic and unpleasant in content, as it contains material from the 'shadow' aspects of the self. Both good and bad dreams promote healing. Healing as a restorative practice takes many forms: we can lance an abscess to let the poison out, a painful but effective procedure, or we can heal in gentler ways. Our western way of life attempts to invalidate the 'shadow' side of ourselves, and hence the shadow is never reconciled. We may learn much from the 'primitive' who pays homage to the devils and demons of the soul. The 'shadow', in Jungian terms, comprises all that which the person refuses or is unable to acknowledge about himself, and so denies and suppresses. In other words, it is the inferior aspect of the personality, the composite of all personal psychic experiences that are incompatible with conscious life. In denying those aspects of the personality, the individual sets up a contrasting, but compensating, splinter aspect of personality that contains both negative and positive traits.

It follows that those aspects of our consciousness which we consider unacceptable will tend to become personified in dreams as shadowy figures that emerge when we let go of consciousness in sleep. We need patience, sensitivity and flexibility to unravel the messages of such dreams, revealing elements of personal shadow patterns of behaviour. While it is difficult to believe that the demons we run from in dreams are a reflection of something deep within our own natures, we can, by using the mirror of dreams, examine such shadow images, and so gain insight. Specifically, Jung said that the 'shadow' of an individual was always of the same sex as him or her, but today we think of 'the shadow' as having contra-sexual shape as well.

Dreams are often filled with childlike images, emotions and fears that we thought we had already dealt with. It is hard sometimes to understand that the tears we shed, as childish imagery touches us in dreams, are the healing tears that are the salve of lifelong wounds. Because the unconscious acts as a storehouse of all our experiences, perhaps even those that we deem prenatal, the past and present become bound together – in a word, atemporal. Hence childhood memories are stirred, unresolved pain and long-forgotten episodes redressed, years later.

Childhood is a time before our present experiences and problems fully separated us from the unconscious landscape. Our own personal childhood is a matter of history, but beyond that is a more primitive, primordial fountainhead of instincts and impulses. During our childhood, we are close to this wellspring of archetypal experience. As adults, we tend to separate from both our personal childhood and the archetypal cradle. Hence impulses and drives can remain infantile throughout adulthood, rising into consciousness only to be denied again and again, when as adults we continually deny their validity.

The more we suppress the more we are distanced from the wellspring of soul and the more our psychic life becomes brittle, colourless and meaningless. Our structured and conditioned lives teach that to be childlike in adult years is wrong, and the paradox of adult life is that in dreams we often look inward and see the inner child. The less we do this in conscious adult life, the more likely it is that primeval and childish imagery will flood our dreams, as the unconscious mind reaches back to our primitive selves to receive guidance and nurturing.

Adults' dreams of childhood serve to heal. Children dream in closer connection to the collective cradle and their dreams are an important focus of psychic health. From the fertility of the collective cradle spring the archetypes awaiting recognition. These are the archetypes with whom the child will form a subjective and lifelong relationship. Simply dismissing a child's dream as nonsense denies their rightful connection. The astrologer who works with children is in a position of great privilege. It is important, when working with children's dreams, not to use adult values for images with which the child is making a subjective connection, but to approach the archetypes cautiously so that the child himself can 'name' it without interference. Small children gain from being encouraged to discuss and even draw their dreams, and in my practice I use blank astrological charts in copious amounts for this purpose.

Jung used the mandala as a way to explore the unconscious. He states:

My mandalas were cryptograms concerning the state of the self which were presented to me anew each day. In them I saw the self – that is, my whole being – actively at work. To be sure, at first I could only dimly understand them; but they seemed to me highly significant, and I guarded them like precious pearls. I had the distinct feeling that they were something central, and in time I acquired through them a living conception of the self. The self, I thought, was like the monad which I am, and which is my world. The mandala represents this monad and corresponds to the microcosmic nature of the psyche.[3]

The mandala of the dream chart is a glimpse of the ever-changing and evolving unconscious level of the self, and when compared with the birth chart presents a new layer of meaning in the process towards individuation. I feel a sense of privilege and awe when a client permits me a peep into their own individuation process.

The connection between dreaming and astrology is as unquestionable as is the partnership between the individual's conscious life journey and astrology—both link us to the principle of linear time and cosmic cycles. Astrologers associate life experience with the transits of the planets. Transits, the orbital movements of planets, do not cease when we sleep, nor does our connectedness with the archetypes of the planets. It is only our *awareness* of experiences that synchronize with the transits that seem to cease with unconsciousness. So, as we experience the transits of the outer planets, patterns emerge and are evident in life experience, and the unconscious attempts to unravel the life experience by dreaming.

The unconscious reflections of day-to-day life, unresolved dilemmas and childhood experiences are all stored material that re-emerges in dreams. 'Messages' synchronize with the positions and transits of planets. Translated into the language of dreams, transits of the planets take on symbolic and pictorial proportions in the unconscious of the dreamer and link with stored material. There is a purpose as well as a meaning for dreaming, and there is a reason why we dream a specific dream at a specific time. We may well ask 'What does the dream mean?', but to explore further with the additional question 'Why did I dream?' opens up a whole new dimension.

In setting up an astrological chart for the time of the dream, we see not only the *what* but the *why* of the dream. We can understand why we slipped into that particular unconscious landscape, if only for a few brief minutes – why the soul aspect of self invited us to explore the sacred space of our own being. There is nothing magical about the dream chart: it is simply a chart of the orbits of the planets and bodies of the solar system in the passage we call transits, but that simple chart represents an important rebirth of some facet of the self. The natal or birth chart in astrology demonstrates the life purpose of the person's journey. The dream chart reflects the unconscious soul purpose in the unfolding of that natal potential.

The emphasis and method of using the dream chart is somewhat different to that used in natal interpretation. By using the dream chart both separately and in conjunction with the natal chart, in a technique of 'synastry', the astrologer achieves a synthesis of the inner and outer experiences of life and of the growth patterns evolving in the dreamer's life. Conscious and unconscious experience, in parallel, is in the astrological synastry between the two charts, and the astrologer is able to perceive individuation as dynamic and active.

Synastry between the dream chart and the natal chart enables us to define the behavioural and response patterns that are being reworked or healed, or are simply in need of attention. The technique will be explained in later chapters, after examination of the meaning of the dream chart and of how it defines the unconscious dynamics in compensating for life's dilemmas. The dream chart allows us to see beyond consciousness for a brief interlude. We experience a time and space when we are unaware of activity on a material level, but are aware of activity on an intangible level. Most importantly, though, the dream chart shows the *intent* of the psyche in choosing to dream a specific dream at a specific time.

I mentioned at the start of this chapter that dreaming can be like observing a drama, and that interpreting the dream by rational means is a natural urge. We take the stance of observer of our dreams and so are like a member of an audience at a private showing. The dream chart is a symbolic stage on which the players are the planets. Some are stars while others play bit parts. All are part of a troupe of interior symbolic Thespians. The chart and the dream contain elements similar to those of a play – cast, plot, scenes, unfolding of the theme, conclusion. The dream chart is the stage, a representation of cast and plot. The dream is the unfolding of the theme and we reach the conclusion and resolution of conflict when we comprehend the plot.

Dreams are not generated specifically by conscious experiences, but by the archetypal energies deeply rooted in the psyche. These energies respond to conscious experiences and synchronize quite clearly with outside happenings. They act by bringing to light, not only the unconscious repercussions of current or past actions, dilemmas and resolutions, but possibly future ones as well. The dream springs from the spontaneous action of the psyche, and its imagery and purpose synchronize with the planets' positions at the time of dreaming. Any provocation then comes from the unconscious dimension.

Dreams are the soul's way of unravelling and attempting to make sense out of the experiences of conscious life. In life, we often get 'off track' and the parallel journeys of worldly activity and soul activity diverge. The dreams we dream are the soul's attempt to realign these paths, using image and form so that they emerge from the psychic depths as mythic and pictorial sequences. We achieve a glimpse of the path in dream. A window to inner perception is then open for a brief time, during which we perceive the workings of the soul in symbolic deeds. The rational and the irrational, the objective and the subjective, the earthly and unearthly, mundane and mystical, profane and sacred are all mirrored components of the self, and the dream lets us see that which we cannot see in our waking hours. As problems emerge and become apparent in daily life, the unconscious tries to unravel past unresolved material, unrecognized present and developing problems, and make sense of the confusion.

The unconscious mind has the task of understanding the language of outer reality in just the same way as we struggle to understand the language of the inner reality. It continually tries to redress the negative experiences of conscious life with the firm intention of healing the damage and moving us into a more compassionate relationship with ourselves. The purpose in dreaming is not so much to find solutions – although, in interpreting the dream we are moved by our natural curiosity to do so – but to understand and integrate, to lead to opportunities for acceptance and let the inner change flow into our worldly lives. In this way we will take appropriate actions, motivated by the unconscious. The mandala of the dream chart is a peep at the ever-changing and evolving self, and presents a layer of the process of being whole.

When astrologers draw up a natal chart, they view the positions of planets along a measure they call the ecliptic. This is the apparent path of the Sun and is represented by the 360° circle of the horoscope. Ancient astrologers divided the circle into twelve divisions, each a constant 30°, which are called 'signs', and these signs coincide with the twelve 'months' of the year. The zodiac is basic to the conscious and world experience. From a geocentric or earth-centred perspective, the centre of the chart is the point from which we view the sky and the movement of the planets, and so the heavens represent our earthly reality. Personal consciousness begins with the birth chart. Planets identify specific drives and personality traits, indicating archetypes or models of behaviour. They correlate with the physical masses of planets and the gods of ancient times. Signs of the zodiac identify the location of planets in the sky and thus in relation to the geocentre, along the ecliptic, and also describe the domain in which the planets' meaning is expressed. As symbolic reference points, the signs are measured from the cycles of equinoxes and solstices that mark our seasons, and have great significance in the manner in which we experience the promise of the birth chart. In natal astrology, signs are said to modify the expression of the planets' significance when they are located within a particular sign meaning and they describe what we might call 'archetypal expectation'. Simply put, we are born with an expectation to experience life in a certain way according to related earth and cosmic patterns, cast at the time of our birth.

Each sign connects to an 'element' – fire, earth, air or water – in a sequential pattern from the 'starting' sign, Aries, which represents the spring equinox in the northern hemisphere, through to Pisces, representing the end of winter. Elements are the essential material of existence, both of the conscious and unconscious, and together combine to create life, so elements are most important in the dream chart, particularly the element that is represented by the sign containing the Moon. (This will be examined later.)

Signs are also described by a 'quality' or 'mode' cardinal, fixed or mutable, also in order from the Aries starting-point. Qualities or modes might be described as worldly standpoints through which the planets' meanings emanate – ways in which the individual experiences worldly life and his attitude to life. They develop and 'group' the signs in two ways: into three consecutive signs representing the seasons, as defined by equinoxes and solstices, and into subgroups in each element. The three signs within the same element group are composed of a cardinal, a fixed and a mutable sign. Each 'cardinal' sign represents a seasonal turning-point – Aries spring, Cancer summer, Libra autumn and Capricorn winter (or the opposite season in the southern hemisphere) – each of which is an equinoctial or solstice point and so represents actual physical and conscious turning-points. In this way cardinal comes to mean generative or creative expression, as something new begins with each season.

In the mid-seasons we have the fixed signs: Taurus, Leo, Scorpio and Aquarius. Their meaning is embedded in fixedness, establishing and preserving, a time of steadiness, growth or sometimes inertia. The third month of a season is represented by mutable signs, and this is a stage where one season ends and another is about to begin. So, mutable signs carry the quality of endings and new beginnings – destruction of the old and seeding of the new – transition to another state of being. These signs are: Gemini, Virgo, Sagittarius and Pisces. All of these paradigms and measures have developed from observable changes in the annual cycle of waking life and so connect more to conscious activity than to unconscious activity, but are reflected by the unconscious as 'inner seasons'.

In addition, astrology has also determined that the planets' expression is modified in certain signs because of 'rulership' by specific planets – being inhibited or enhanced, according to which planet rules the sign. This is referred to as being 'dignified', 'exalted', in 'detriment' or 'fall', and from this the natal astrologer evaluates how the planet expresses its meaning through a 'tonal quality', whether it is repressed or freed from the boundaries of sign meaning. In the unconscious there are no such boundaries. We are born with a certain propensity to experience life in a particular way, and this propensity is reinforced and actuated by our life experience, so that the planet's expression becomes habituated in the individual's world. In some ways this restricts the individual from accessing the full potential of the planet.

Most of these old terms do not apply in dream astrology, although the elements, as the essence of life both conscious and unconscious, *are* of great significance in the dream chart, and the quality and other factors should be considered to apply more to the natal or conscious application of the planet. Thus, when working with the dream chart, if the planet Venus is in the sign Aries, it should be understood that the planet is in the intuitive element of fire, vital, instinctual and active, rather than that it might be 'debilitated' because it is in 'detriment'. For this reason, throughout this book, little reference is made to signs except to define the element or in understanding the 'houses'. We may use the traditional paradigms in the astrology of consciousness, but in dream charts the planets are more 'open' to express their meaning in an unconditioned way.

There is no 'detriment' in the unconscious – the Venus factor may well *seem* to be disadvantaged in conscious life, but in the unconscious landscape of dreams it is intuitive, exciting, vibrant and decisive in the elemental fire! There is no 'fixedness' in dreams – only the reflected fixedness of the dreamer's conscious life and attitude. Dreams reveal the fullness and glory of the planets' archetypal richness, without limit. In this way, when the nun dreamed of being a harlot, she was experiencing the sensual, Venus part of her personality in the fullness of its symbolism, not just in terms that are consistent with her habitual conscious expectation. When the time was appropriate, the unconscious brought more fullness into her life, more knowledge and compassionate understanding of her potential.

Limited and controlled as we tend to be by our expectations in waking life, we are astonished at the imagery invoked in dreams. We 'do' things we cannot imagine with our conscious minds. We declare, 'I never dreamed I was capable of such a thing!', but we are indeed capable of all we dream, were we not so constricted. Conscious experience reveals only a facet of a planet's meaning, limited to, and confirmed and reinforced by, natal expectations. So, the nun is experiencing Venus in a way that is quite inconsistent with her conscious understanding. The dream chart can reveal specifically which area of her whole life experience could be the richer through this encounter. What an adventure each dream is, and what an opportunity to see our limited expectations open up and reach for full experience! This is the quintessence of real growth. For example, if Mars, representing the self-determining and assertive factor in the psyche, is not validated or fully confirmed in life, and consequently loses its impetus, then its impetus is relegated to the shadow area in the unconscious. You should not then be surprised that in dreams you can experience its full primeval, forceful, savage and barbaric expression. It is unlimited in soul experience!

The natal chart reveals the potential for whole psychic life, as it shows the cycles and unfolding patterns of a much greater macrocosm, but it seems we only consciously experience individual expression according to the pattern at the moment of birth. It defines our *life's intent* within a framework of a greater universal intent. Structured life and social and family conditioning are specific to consciousness. Archetypal expectations are reinforced by activities and relationships, and further distance us from our true spiritual and universal connection. Conscious life reveals only facets of the potential in life. The broad scope inherent in the core planetary significance becomes more restricted, cloaked in the layer of personal meaning as time goes by. We tend to act out our lives automatically, unaware of the enormous potential available to us in the unconscious.

Dreams reveal that rich potential. In dreams we can reach back to the entire archetypal time–space realm and experience that realm in ways that may seem alien to our conscious understanding, but which are strangely comforting and familiar at the time we are dreaming. The seemingly prophetic dream as a phenomenon is the intuitive dimension of the unconscious self's ability to pre-empt and anticipate the future. When the nun dreams of being a harlot, when the bride dreams of throwing lamb chops at passing prostitutes, when the loving mother dreams she sacrifices her child to a volcano or the stereotypical spinster feels horrified to find her dreams a rich pageant of sexual athletics, they all tap into the rich pageant of potential in the unlimited realm of the cosmos. Such promise is represented astrologically by the planets, signs, houses and aspects of charts.

The dream chart is a powerful mandala of inner life, unrestricted by natal expectation. It links us to the soul's journey. Each dream remembered and timed is a pivotal point where the conscious and unconscious meet. Linear time regulates our conscious activities but there is no linear time in dreams. So we may have dreams which have no apparent connection to current daily life but hark back to previous problems and themes, or forward to some developmental phase of the self. Linear time – time that is forward and backward – does not apply, except in defining the conscious manifestation of the dream. The unconscious establishes the link as it transposes its circulating time into linear conscious time through the phenomenon of remembering.

We may dream, according to Dr C. G. Jung, constantly. 'It is very probable,' he says, 'that we dream continually, only our consciousness makes such a noise in the waking state that we no longer hear it ... if we could keep a continuous record we should see that the whole process follows a definite trend.'[4] Transits of the Sun, Moon, and planets are happening all the time, but often the wider astrological significance of major transits will 'make such a noise' that the momentary ones are drowned out. Awareness of a dream significant enough to overcome the noise of consciousness must then synchronize with significant transits, however brief. Soul continually seeks to redress the ravages of consciousness with the intention of compensating and getting us 'back on track', and so selects a proper time when we can remember and bring the dream into awareness.

Synthesizing the dream chart with the natal chart allows us to distinguish the particular expression of our psychic life in the process of becoming individuated. This comparison of charts, called synastry, is a way to observe, not just the major cosmic events in the individual life, but the momentary contacts made by those bodies not generally used in the study of transits, and to see their significance as revealed in the dream.

Houses are most important in the dream chart. They mark the time at which the dream is born into consciousness. The moment we awake and try to understand the dream we are giving it form. It is consciousness of the dream that gives us insight into what is occurring in the unconscious. In choosing the time to bring the dream into conscious awareness, the mandala as a circumambulation of the self is suspended and quantified. The great round ceases momentarily. This is the basis on which we work with the dream in linear, conscious life. Understanding the houses of astrology will help to define this, and house connections will be explored.

'Aspects' (angular relationships) between planets as interrelationships between types of behaviour are significant in the dream chart in exactly the same way as in the natal chart – aspects describe the quality of the relationship. Some aspects are defined as harmonious, or soft. Specific aspects in the dream chart will be explained in detail in Chapter 7. Traditionally the soft aspects used in astrology are the trine, the sextile and the quintile, and some conjunctions. So-called hard aspects are the square, the opposition, quincunx and sesquisquare, and some conjunctions, and they imply, in dreams, a statement, dilemma or lack of ease. The soft aspects are those which are appropriate to healing, to the pleasurable and sometimes humorous and reconciling energies. Hard aspects are the more defined, clear-cut messages which focus on underlying habitual thought patterns and behaviour, and so are sharp aspects leading to discovery through challenge. We might say that the hard aspects are the signposts of the dream and the soft aspects the landscape.

In interpreting the aspects shown in the dream chart, it is those aspects created by the Moon and Mercury with other planets that are of primary importance. These two bodies have enormous import in the dream chart. The fastest-moving body in the sky is the Moon and, when in direct motion, the second fastest is Mercury. The Moon's light is a constant waxing and waning of the world of brightness and the world of darkness. The speed at which it travels the zodiac will mean that in twenty-four hours it will appear to pass through all the houses. The Moon as a timing device is essential to the dream chart, for it is the Moon's timing that lights the house that represents some fragment of hidden psychic wholeness; imagine that the Moon conspires with the solar dimensions of time to ensure that the dream is dreamed at the appropriate time. The Moon's position in a house lights that area of psychic experience, and aspects made by the Moon to planets illuminate some facet of the core experience of that planet, without message or judgement. Also imagine the Moon as entering into an allegorical contract with Mercury, the symbol of mind, to highlight and illuminate the imagery in dreams.

Mercury represents the mental function that creates the language of dreams and carries messages. Mercury's role in the dream drama is primarily as narrator and secondarily as healer, both in the name of that which the Moon floods with light. In the dream chart, it is the aspects of Mercury to other planets that will enable us to define both the language and the message. Mercury translates the meaning of the planets it aspects into dream symbols, and speaks their language through imagery. In the next chapter we examine the function of Mercury as mental activity, soul guide, translator and healer. As we enter a dream we experience a journey, we pass over a metaphorical bridge, leaving behind, in true humility, all that is important in daily life. Sleeping, with only the mental function seeming active, body awareness suspended, we are, in a sense, in the mystical presence of *Hermes Psychopompos* – Soul Guide – the guide to the underworld in Greek mythology. We experience the underworld of our selves in all its potential, we experience personal soul and contact soul dimensions of the collective (what Dr Jung defines as *anima mundi*, or world soul), leaving traces of our presence. We make a return journey to wakefulness and may then re-examine considerations we once held so dear and find we no longer value them as we did.

2

Mercury –
Guide to the Dream Journey

Nowhere can a man find a quieter or more untroubled retreat than in his own soul.

Marcus Aurelius

Mercury is the planet that represents the capacity to think, to communicate, transmit and disseminate information that stems both from our own internally derived ideas and from those that come to us externally, in written, verbal, auditory, physical or visual form. Astrologically, Mercury is connected to the signs Gemini and Virgo, the third and sixth houses, and the elements air and earth. Without the capacity to think, we cannot have any sort of life; to be brain-dead is to be finally dead. Scientifically, even though the heart has stopped beating, it is only when the brain dies or ceases to emit any electrical impulse that we have no more worldly existence. Our ability to think is paramount at all stages of and in all aspects of living, both conscious, ego-oriented living and unconscious, soul-oriented living. It follows then that this planet is most powerful and vital because it has the versatility of meaning and the flexibility to act at all levels of being.

Mercury's faculty seems to be in place before birth, as experiments show a foetus responds to external stimuli as early as three months' gestation. The first cry of the newborn is the confirmation of the Mercury capacity to vocalize. Its thrashing arms and legs confirm its capacity to move and use the limbs that will later take it places and enable it to craft, to write and to gesture. As the baby grows it becomes observant, aware of its environment, and the parent can watch its growing awareness as it learns to process information that comes to it through its senses.

These are the observable developments in our Mercurial abilities and for every perceptible development there is an equal but imperceptible interchange taking place as Mercury stores information in the deepest recesses of the psyche and mediates conscious thinking. Mercury in the psyche is always dual in nature. It has the dexterity to access another language, the language of symbol. Symbol comes to us from collective sources stored as ancient memories, often distorted by time and certainly affected by historical and tribal expectations. Symbol has no relationship with our conscious communication. The unconscious 'speaks' through symbols and Mercury gives us the capacity to understand such symbols, not in a rational, external way, but intuitively, using that sixth sense so often neglected in conscious life. It is through symbol that we reach the fullness of our psychic potential, and dreams are, in effect, created and translated by the competence of Mercury. Jolande Jacobi quotes Jung: 'Whether something is a symbol depends on the attitude of the consciousness that contemplates it; the question is whether the individual has the aptitude or the disposition to perceive an object, a tree for example, not merely as a concrete phenomenon but as a symbol for something more or less unknown and vitally meaningful, a symbol of human life.'[1]

Everyone, to some degree or other, and especially the astrologer and those who work in fields where there is a search for meaningful and soulful connection, has this 'aptitude and disposition'.[2] We can see this emerging in the dialogue of a dream told to me by Kelly. 'I felt something in my throat, and pushed my hand into my mouth and pulled out what seemed to be a plastic bag, which was filled with squiggly things, some red, some white. They were like worms, or veins, some were dead, some were alive. I realized it had a root that still remained in my throat, so I cut it off, but felt I had left something behind.'

In this dream there is both allegory and symbol. Allegory connects indirect but associated ideas, by expressing something with a known content, in an imaginative and sometimes pictorial way. Symbol contains an unknown quality, an archetypal core, which gives it a meaning which cannot always be expressed in rational terms. It carries an archetypal value of its own, and has no verbal or rational equivalent. Symbol is reached only through imagination, fantasy and intuition. The allegory is in the action of something choking Kelly — there is an active story here, couched in analogy. We can understand that whatever is being withheld, or is stuck in her throat, needs examination. The symbol is in the contents of her throat. There is a vitality in the plastic bag as a container; the veins or worms might represent symbols of life and death that defy interpretations beyond the feelings and image that they evoke.

Using the techniques that will be explained throughout this book, Kelly and I together were able to see that Kelly's communicative faculties, early

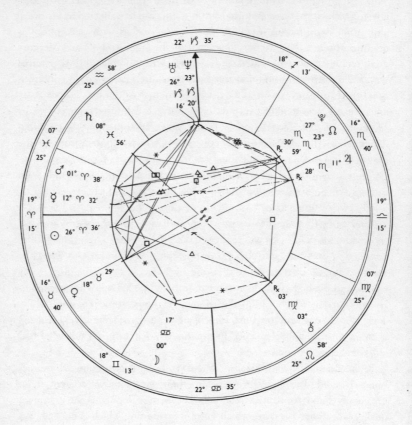

1. Kelly's Blob Dream (illustrating the role of Mercury)

education, environmental factors in her intellectual development, spiritual ideals and visions were all involved in the dream. The past with its secrets and unresolved pain is involved. These matters tie in to early learning, to moral and ethical imprints that have been conditioned by parental influences. Guided by the chart, Kelly explored the basis of her early learning through family life and education and the ways in which she was taught to speak and communicate. The imprinted messages of her early family life, translated into feelings and symbols, are a potent expression of this dream. The dream chart indicates the need for further exploration and reveals that her childhood, while outwardly 'respectable' and socially correct, was filled with arguments, differing religious attitudes within the household and enormous fear of a stepfather, whose verbal condemnation and dictatorial attitude towards Kelly at an early age prompted intense anger and fear. The subliminal insecurities centre on speaking out or expressing opinions, for the child Kelly feared for her life when, at table – a time when families gather and conversation should be encouraged – she was hit with the back of a knife for 'opening her mouth'. The symbol of the plastic bag emerged as fears which the infant Kelly could not articulate, but had absorbed, stored and held over into adult life, fears which were now illustrated in the dream symbol – unspoken and unexpressed rage of childhood, some still 'alive'. Communicative factors, morality and the religious and ethical dilemma indicated by the dream chart show in the conditioned attitude that 'the parent is always right' and 'God doesn't love children who are not obedient.' The metaphor of the 'bag of worms' indicates that Kelly is still reluctant or unable to articulate her anger lest she invoke the wrath of family. 'A root was left behind,' and she used a knife to cut it off.

The stepfather is no longer alive, so there can be no confrontation, no conscious resolution or articulation of feelings, and therefore it seems that Kelly must continue to carry the pain of her childhood, but only in part, for the main catharsis has occurred in the dream, with only remnants left behind. Kelly has an excellent voice and around the time of the dream had been offered an opportunity to perform as a singer with a band. She felt reluctant as, in the past, she has experienced stage fright, saying that she felt like a vulnerable child when called on to perform in this way. She is also exploring spiritual studies to try to reconcile some of her early teachings.

Kelly saw the dream as 'bringing out the worms', ridding herself of the block that inhibits both her performance and her articulation of spiritual matters, and so was able to examine, rationalize and evaluate the childhood pain and her childhood inability to communicate her own thoughts, ethics and feelings. When the symbol of that pain was brought into consciousness and its context understood, an aspect of Kelly's life was healed.

Mercury enables us to integrate what is commonly called the left and right brain function. It enables us to assimilate, process, store and recall information, resulting in our being able to learn from experiences, enjoy our capacity for both definitive and abstract thought and then act upon it. It empowers us to access intuition, use imagination and symbolism, and transcend the boundaries of time with forethought and afterthought.

The left side of the brain is said to control the right side of the body and handle information and thoughts in an analytical, logical and rational fashion. The left brain recalls information into consciousness and breaks perceptions into components, handling each component as a separate entity, not as part of a whole. Left-brain meaning is focused on details, not on a relationship between parts, and so thoughts are sequential, neither overlapping nor simultaneous. The left brain interprets speech, and leans towards the mathematical and rational. It is this Mercurial action that takes up much of our waking hours. It is the left brain that is responsible for learned or conditioned behaviour and thinking, and for routine and explicit knowledge. The right brain, on the other hand, by seeing things in their entirety, apparently is capable of handling multiple operations simultaneously, but not sequentially. Right-brain activity is holistic and non-rational, takes the component parts and organizes them into a whole through imagination. This is intuitive rather than factual activity because the right brain is not aware of the component realities in their factual sense but uses other sources, sounds, smells and so on, that all register as a collection of the whole. It is the right brain that is responsible for appreciation of artistry through feelings and for intuitive and abstract knowledge.

It is tempting to try to divide the rational/definitive and the non-rational/abstract capabilities of the mind, the implication being that they operate independently, or to assume that the unconscious mind works less clearly than the conscious. The two do, however, operate simultaneously and have equal value. It is only through a chosen perspective or predisposition that we might tend to favour one over the other. Graham Dunstan Martin explains: 'One might think that the "abstract" should be equated with the "tacit" and the "concrete" with the "explicit" in the sense that you can see reality clearly, whereas you perceive abstractions only dimly. On the contrary.

Clarity is not the test. The "abstract", though often brilliantly clear, is what one can never touch, while the "concrete", though often darkly mysterious, is what one touches all the time.'[3] Both halves of the brain, the dual Mercury function, allow us to experience an unblocked flow of thoughts and this gives us the ability to construct and define, to bring into consciousness all the symbols, visions, thoughts and ideas embedded in the unconscious. We are simply inclined to be more clear on the left-brain, definitive function during our waking hours and on the right-brain operations, wordless and imaginal, in dreams.

Jung relates a wonderful story illustrating the mind's capacity for simultaneous action.

During the meal I was sitting opposite a middle-aged gentleman with a long handsome beard, who had been introduced to me as a barrister. We were having an animated conversation about criminal psychology. In order to answer a particular question of his, I made up a story to illustrate it, embellishing it with all sorts of details. While I was telling my story, I noticed a quite different expression came over the man's face and a silence fell on the table. Very much abashed, I stopped speaking. Thank heavens we were already at the dessert, so I soon stood up and went into the lounge of the hotel. There I withdrew into a corner, lit a cigar and tried to think over the situation. At this moment one of the other guests who had been sitting at my table came over and asked reproachfully, 'How did you ever come to commit such a frightful indiscretion?' 'Indiscretion?' 'Why, yes, that story you told.' 'But I made it all up!' To my horror and amazement it turned out that I had told the story of the man opposite me, exactly and in all its details. I also discovered, at this moment, that I could not remember a single word of the story – even to this day I have been unable to recall it.[4]

It is important to remember the constant duality of the mind. In the astrology of dreaming Mercury accesses parts *and* whole, actual *and* imaginative, constantly transmitting information from, so to speak, 'above' to 'below', and vice versa. Mind is Mercury – Mercury is mind – our very reality depends entirely on being able to make associations with both the external and internal worlds.

We enter a dream as though we were part of an audience, watching with inner eyes as the play unfolds its meaning. We have no understanding of the plot or the direction that the drama will take but, aware that something is evolving, we enter without resistance. Slipping into the dream state is an enigmatic experience, a sea journey into the depths of the psychic soul dimension.

There is no scientific way to capture or measure that moment between waking and sleep, that transition from consciousness to dream – in the blink of an eye, the mystical curtain draws back and the stage is revealed. We have only a vague awareness of the unconscious as a separate realm whose dimension and scope has no physical nature, the reaches of which are accessed in sleep; our minds move from conscious, ego-oriented life to soul life in an instant. The inner landscape of the self is a realm where images and dreams are far beyond the scope of conscious experience. They have evolved and have been brought to us through our ancestral heritage, and are personally experienced in our symbol-making, through dreams as well as through imaging, meditating and contemplative stillness.

Personal soul is an intrinsic part of, and is shaped by, the ancestral and collective patterns of the universal soul. Universal soul is undifferentiated in content and shape, made up of images, mythic and cultural, vivid and vaporous, a living entity that has its own intent and does not serve conscious concerns. Through dreaming we are able to discover the archetypal images that inhabit this dimension called the collective unconscious. We begin to move away from the dependence of conscious life and reconnect with the universal reality as we enter the dream. Dreams express soul. The dream drama is to psychic, inner reality as our conscious drama is to daily, outer reality. The two realities are quite distinct and separate, yet indivisible and inexorably linked.

It is through the magic of Mercury that we can lead conscious lives which are truly free, for dreams provoke us into making choices and decisions, and give us the capacity to look forward and backward, outward and inward, and to live rich and full lives here on earth. Mercury is the constant by which we attune our worldly identity and by which we can explore our immaterial soul identity. As we sleep, it shows that which has given substance to our past, present and future; all our perceived realities and all that has been repressed and contained within the subconscious is refined here. Mercury, is the guide of the psyche, negotiating the mystical, unknown, yet strangely familiar landscape – and is also the ideal of healing, effecting spiritual rebirth through contact with our symbolic selves and bringing such healing back to consciousness, where it helps to reconcile the parts of our divided self.

Mercury's importance in the dream chart cannot be overstated. Its place-ment in the dream chart, its aspects to other planets and to those in the natal chart will be the means by which we can begin to understand the message that comes to us from ourselves. The mental process is used in deciphering what dimension of soul is being metamorphosed and why the dream chose us at that particular time. An alchemical change occurs with every dream. If we know this, we can take comfort and return with an inner awareness and a healthful attitude, knowing that the balance is partially redressed, some part of the process of individuation enhanced.

The dream chart and its synastry with the birth chart offers immediate insight into the purpose of the dream and allows us to discuss and understand the divided parts of the whole, and learn something of their strengths and weaknesses. In this way the astrologer can assist and empower the dreamer to heal the breaches. Comprehension rather than interpretation is the aim in examining dreams. By accessing feelings, comprehension becomes knowledge. Knowledge promotes growth. Specific interpretation does nothing more than make bald statements that promote no knowledge or growth, but remain static and stagnant. Through the fragmentary 'little hidden door'[5] we glimpse a numinous portion of the psyche of another and we should treat this personal connection with the utmost respect. Each dream is unique to the dreamer, despite the emergence of collective symbols common to all humanity. No arbitrary method of interpretation can possibly reveal the meaning for the individual, but the individual who explores the dream may learn much about his own psychic make-up.

Mercury gives us the ability to converse with others — to express ideas and to impress those ideas on the mind of another. The dream content allows the astrologer to guide his client, to accompany that person through a process of investigating the unconscious inner realm of his psyche. In doing so, understanding the reason why the unconscious has chosen this time to produce the dream assists in guiding the client to a fuller understanding and knowledge of his self. The dream chart empowers one to do so. Its mandala is a map of the dream; it plots signposts of the inner landscape and directs the way for exploration.

Understanding the language of one's dreams is an exercise in lateral thinking, and in the study of allegory and symbol. These are the paths which Mercury opens, and through the dream chart we can trace the message of the symbols. The aspects that Mercury makes to other planets will reveal the message of the dream. Aspects are the relationships, however brief, that connect the meaning embedded in the symbolism of the planets. Planets touch each other and, when their aspects involve Mercury, the mind receives and transmits information in accord with the individual principle of the other planet. Any contract between Mercury and another planet creates a dialogue between the mind and whatever that planet represents as an active part of the personality. When using the dream chart, we might imagine a personified Mercury speaking on behalf of that planet.

Mercury in Aspect to the Sun

Mercury is never more than 28° away from the sun, so the only significant aspect it will make in the dream chart is a superior or inferior conjunction. The focus will be on the waking self, the role the dreamer plays in life, his ego and identity, and the course of his mundane life's path. Because the Sun represents how we perceive ourselves, and in some respects the ego, it is as though Mercury and the Sun together create a lens to focus on the conscious side of life. Any message is about some aspect of the ego in its relationship with conscious activity. Mercury, in the dream state, will connect and focus on the intelligent, rational function of the mind in the waking state. Images and symbols will have an objective meaning, particular to the way in which the dreamer perceives his own reality, his lifestyle and worldly activities, and his relationships with the outside world. The dream may indicate a need for a change of thinking at the conscious level, perhaps in outlook or persona attitudes. Some facet of recent or current activities or relationships is addressed in the dream, or it may simply confirm that the dreamer is on the right track.

The message may be one that initiates decisive action on waking, or suggests future directions. It can also indicate that the dreamer is in some way preoccupied with himself, is restless or needs to think about attitudes and directions that are affecting his general way of life. Simultaneous aspects Mercury makes to other planets will give some indication of the connotations, of what those planets mean, to the conscious self, but the Mercury–Sun conjunction will effectively focus with clarity on 'real' and personal dimensions of life. Other aspects will be a part of that focus in waking life, and the principles of those other planets may remind the dreamer to take personal control in regard to the meaning of those planets in his life. For example, if Mercury is conjunct the Sun and opposes Pluto, there is a call from the subconscious for enormous change at some level of conscious activity.

Mercury in Aspect to the Moon

When Mercury is in aspect to the Moon, it is in contact with the body that represents the inner, unconscious and reflective nature of the dreamer. The mind in the dream is subject to the emotional self, and expresses an uneasy combination of thinking and feeling. In contrast to its contacts with the Sun, Mercury's contact with the Moon will speak of the inner, sentient, inscrutable facets of life. The message is from the moody, changeable and non-rational side of the personality, and has nothing to do with reason or the logical mind. Dreams are sensitized by experiences often long forgotten by the conscious mind, but imprinted on the psyche – the emotional experiences in childhood. Well-being and health, feelings, relationships of an emotional kind, the ecstasy and anguish of love and loss are all presented in symbolic form for rational understanding. The mind is in touch with the storehouse of all that has been experienced in life and has filtered into the unconscious, and so unresolved feelings emerge in the allegory and images of the dream. There is a subtle interchange between thinking and feeling that is often constrained in worldly life, so feelings, moods, reactions that have been curbed will be a feature of dreams. Such dreams will rarely provoke action, but rather the acceptance and healing of tensions in relationships with others. Such dreams can be inspirational, creative and profoundly informative of inner potentials for a more soulful life. Common aspects to other planets will involve the emotional, subjective connotations of those other planets. The lunar side of the personality does not provoke, it does not imply action, but produces images that represent nurturing, sentiments, habits, prejudices or infantile patterns of behaviours that are in some way reworked in the dream. Mercury in aspect to the Moon promotes emotional healing through acceptance of the message, and opens a channel for comprehending our emotional nature and the way in which it affects our daily lives.

Mercury in Aspect to Venus

These two planets, because of their astronomical orbits, are never more than 74° apart in the chart, so the widest contact they can make is the quintile aspect and all those that lie within that angular arc; the conjunction, sextile, septile and novile being those used in the astrology of the dream chart. This implies that the relationship between the two, their 'marriage', is one of harmony. It is likely that other, more potent, hard aspects are operating at the time, but it is not inconceivable that an aspect between these two planets in the principal Mercury aspect of the dream chart may become the main conduit for the mind. Venus brings matters of value, legality, personal truth, affection and fair exchange to the imagery of the dream, along with matters connecting with affections, idealism, art, creativity, pleasure, healing, love, relationships of a loving or intimate nature, and feelings.

Dreams can be delightful expressions of the humorous and compassionate nature of the dreamer and put the dreamer in touch with the less ponderous and difficult aspects of conscious existence. Such dreams bring a lightness in imagery that is refreshing and healing, may mirror the truth about something in life and may provoke the dreamer to re-evaluate some part of his conscious life and take himself less seriously. Tact, diplomacy and the persuasive faculties of the personality are demonstrated in the dream and may motivate the person to take a different approach in his dealings with others in daily life, to relax more, enjoy the pleasurable aspects of life or see a different perspective on some dilemma. When there are aspects from the Moon to other planets as well, the Mercury–Venus aspect will act to lighten and heal what might emerge as a more direct theme in the dream, so it is always worth observing this contact for a sub-theme that is potentially mollifying.

Mercury in Aspect to Mars

Here there is a combination of self-will and the mind, linked in the manner of the aspect in a forceful and penetrating way. Dream imagery is often bloody, combative, incisive and clear-cut, and there is little subtlety in the message, which, although it is composed of symbols, nevertheless contains a direct statement. Mercury 'speaks' from the part of the self that is decisive, self-actuating, contentious and often angry. Mars symbolizes personal ambitions and objectives, and the capacity to be energetic in the pursuit of those goals. The message is often understood quickly, intuitively, but is not always acceptable to the waking self. Through the lens of will and mind, Mercury is bringing a personal message about action. Mars is the component of the self that will decide clearly whether or not to spend time and energy, and so the message can indicate that the time is right to confront specific facets of consciousness, to move to promote some angle in life's experience or to take evasive action.

The message is purposefulness, keeping an eye on the target – success in worldly activities — by acting on the dream message. There can also be a warning for caution, if matters of the ego have become too inflated, and other aspects together with this one might give some indication of how this occurs. The mind, with Mars, is acutely aware, quick, facile and aggressive. Those dreamers who are unable to express their anger in daily life often have dreams where the anger is graphically expressed. This in itself is cathartic and healing, a release valve of tension, and so helps the dreamer to deal with the need to be passive or self-sacrificing in life. However, too many such dreams, while beneficially cathartic, might imply that conscious action will have to be taken eventually. Sexuality and sexual appetites, eroticism, passions and goals, can all feature in the dreams when Mercury contacts Mars.

Mercury in Aspect to Jupiter

Jupiter represents the urge to expand and grow at all levels of life   to achieve more, be more, have more and give more, and to gain more meaningful interaction at all levels of development — intellectually, materially, spiritually, emotionally, physically and socially, all within the paradigms of an honourable ethic for living. Jupiter encourages and opens the mind to all the wide and sweeping potential of the dream allegory. The lens of Mercury—Jupiter is intellectual and intuitive, and is not always clearly expressed in the dream message, but may be cloaked in colourful meaning that can confuse or distract from the main point. The message is often about social and moral matters, ethical and legal judgements and opinions expressed in daily life. It connects to conditioned and entrenched hierarchical and family ethics and morals, as well as to learned intellectual matters.

It might point directly to where the dreamer is inflating his ideals and capabilities, being arrogant, high-handed or presumptive, or where he is not developing and needs to take some steps to open up, change direction and grow. It brings the opportunity through the dream to see the comical side of the self, for Jupiter's capacity for the ribald, the hilarious, the jovial, is channelled through the mind so that self-importance, self-aggrandizement is seen, unconsciously, in its most ridiculous guise. If the attitude in daily life is puritanical or judgemental, we see in the dream the truth of our attitudes towards life. Aspects made to other planets will become enlarged and elaborated by the aspect to Jupiter, so it often serves to emphasize the other aspects involved with Mercury—Jupiter — to make sure they are noticed through the bright and numinous imagery of the dreams. Jupiter opens the mind to all possibilities, both positive and negative, and any simultaneous aspects to other planets will indicate where psychological and worldly growth might take place, or where there is an exaggerated sense of self-importance.

Mercury in Aspect to Saturn

This contact brings out facets of inner and outer life that are entrenched and ingrained. Saturn represents the capacity to regulate, refine and discipline the self wisely, but negatively represents patterns of behaviour that can be melancholic, restricting and discouraging. When Mercury speaks Saturn's language, imagery often reflects some ancestral pattern of behaviour or attitude, learned and reinforced in life through social experience. Family and its regulatory attitudes arise in these dreams, and the mind is prompted to reconsider the relative values of such paradigms.

Habits and self-defeating mechanisms in the psyche can be symbolically presented in the dream and, as the Saturn part of the personality represents the various stages of maturing and ageing, these dreams often coincide with crossroads and turning-points in psychic life. They focus on the need to harvest the valuable and to prune and refine what is no longer relevant in whole-life experience. The negative connotation of this connection is in depressing and suppressing what is presented in the dream imagery because the dilemma, as perceived in conscious life, is so large that a waking solution cannot be found. In this case the dream will recur again at another time, and the initial dream serves to alert the dreamer to the need for acceptance or for change to the conscious limiting factors. The positive connotation is inner wisdom and mature standing within society's framework. The rational mind is stimulated into reviewing life, its successes and failures, how limitations might have come from some base of fear or loneliness, or have been imprinted by social expectations, experience and traditions; how personal and family taboos inhibit growth, as do unresolved painful experiences. These powerful dreams bring to the dreamer a sense of their own authority together with sacred collective knowledge. They bring the potential for healing by empowering the dreamer to step beyond the boundaries of regulated conscious life and strike a balance between the past and the future potentialities of the whole self.

Mercury in Aspect to Uranus

When Mercury is connected to Uranus, the mind is excited and amazed by provocative imagery which is often bizarre and disjointed. The dream imagery is representative of all one's inner potential for creative, ingenious and original thought, as well as all that is disconnective and unstable.

Progressive and innovative ideas appear in the dream imagery as 'a bolt from the blue'. Such dreams connect with the anarchistic, lawless and chaotic side of the personality. They might invoke images that are seemingly destructive and so act as a release valve for the unconscious desire to rock the boat, or to shatter some aspect of the status quo as it is represented in the dreamer's worldly life. In doing so, awareness of some facet of life that needs to change is brought to the dreamer. These are dreams that provoke a change of mind-set, as they offer alternatives encapsulated in the images and symbols of the dreams. They serve to indicate, like a warning bell, that things are not as they seem. The status quo in worldly life is too limiting. The revolutionary spirit is strong, as is the desire to be self-willed and independent, and the dream highlights this facet of psychic development. Simultaneous aspects will indicate what component of worldly life might, subliminally, be identified as in need of change. In dreaming Mercury–Uranus dreams, dreamers are aware of being 'outside of the self', and so the perspective is objective, unemotional in the main, and the dream can be analysed logically, for often the dream makes sense even during dreaming! Time is transcended in these dreams, so clairvoyant dreams are not uncommon under this aspect and, given an inventive approach to the symbolic language, can be a very useful tool in making decisions and changes in conscious life. The insight that comes through these dreams is worthy of note and often coincides with cycles in life when decision and change, both materially and in attitude, are a feature.

Mercury in Aspect to Neptune

Neptune represents that part of the self that is idealistic, disconnected from materialism, illusionary and deceptive. Representing the capacity to dream in all its implications, Neptune brings the attributes of imagination and spirituality to the self. When these two planets are in contact the dream symbols are obscure, shadowy and indistinct. Feelings are invoked in dreams where Mercury speaks Neptune's language, and exploration of the feelings experienced in the dream will be as valuable as an attempt to rationalize such a dream. The mind is confused by Neptune and the dream seems to be seen through a mist. Negatively, such dreams can invoke feelings of victimization, inexplicable fear and even paranoia, and can also speak of addictive or self-deceptive tendencies in consciousness. The lies the dreamer tells himself, or the lies others tell him that he chooses to believe, can be reflected back in the dream and there clarified. The Mercury–Neptune aspect challenges the dreamer to try to sort out the truth of his inner and outer perceptions of the world. The dreams may indicate some areas in life that are unrealistic in worldly terms and unattainable in reality unless there is a shift in perspective. Thus the dream might symbolically indicate ways in which the waking dream might be attained by such a shift. It may tell the dreamer to wake up to his or her reality. Positively, it can have an inspirational quality, particularly in the dreams of those who are already living soulful lives, aware of the depth of waking symbols in daily activities. Artists and writers might dream their next work as imagination and mind connect. Hidden potential in psychic development emerges as the mind is able to circumvent the blockages and limitations of mundane life, linear time and the boundaries of the known world, and hence gain access to visionary and other-worldly facets of the self.

Mercury in Aspect to Pluto

Pluto is representative of that part of the personality that is most deeply hidden in the shadow aspects of the self. Dreams reveal the darkest side of the personality as well as the potential brightness in the shadow. Pluto connects with life and death, and Hermes/Mercury was the mediator between the upper air and the realm of Pluto – Hades – in myth. As Psychopompos, he guided the souls of the dead to the underworld.

The struggle to individuate is perhaps most profound in these dreams, as it seems that the intensity of the dream indicates that there is a facet of psychic development that must be overcome before progress can be made. When Mercury brings a message to the mind from the shadow part of the personality, the dream is vivid with quite disturbing images. Effectively, the dream is a revived facet of life's experience or an unacknowledged negative quality in the dreamer's nature, and demands that the dreamer work to understand what indeed has been resurrected from the deepest reaches of the psyche. There are few 'easy' dreams with a Pluto contact because what emerges cannot easily be reburied; images will return in waking hours and must be dealt with. Such dreams are often the seeds by which conscious work in dealing with shadow issues in life are provoked. The dream we examined on p. 20, Kelly's dream, is just such a dream, as Mercury is sesquisquare Pluto, and this dream brought images that have a mythic quality. It invoked images of the task of Heracles, in his struggle with the Hydra, in which he tried to chop off the regenerating heads. This can be interpreted as the struggle of ego and shadow. A bloody struggle, for each time Heracles cut off one of the heads of the Hydra, it regrew. At last Heracles cauterized each head as it was cut off; he held up the heads to the light, whereupon they were transformed into jewels. So it is when Mercury contacts Pluto – some aspect of the darkness needs to be brought into the light, so that it no longer has the power to harm. Images can be demonic, monstrous and nightmarish, and force the dreamer to confront them. When Mercury brings to the mind a message from Pluto, it is bringing a message of potential healing and transformation from the forgotten or deeply suppressed side of nature, but Pluto asks that it be faced and recognized.

Mercury in Aspect to Chiron

Chiron is the part of the self that is hurt, wounded by alienation, abandonment and the pain of rejection; it is the seat of injured instincts and drives, but it is also that aspect of the self that is capable of self-healing, and of healing others. Negatively it is that urge that is capable of wounding, of being the perpetrator of injury as well as being victimized. Old pain, childhood wounds and the ways in which the dreamer might have immortalized and nursed such woundedness are brought to the mind's attention. The sense of aliena-tion from the collective in worldly activities, of being apart from peers and unable to reach out because of the fear of rejection is symbolically represented by aspects to Chiron. There may also be a predisposition for holding on, emotionally, to painful experiences in order to justify some attitude or avoid some action, so that the dreamer is often confronted, not only with his own wounded self but with his own part in the perpetuation of that wound. The dreamer is often confronted with pictures that reflect the psychosomatic nature of illness. Positively, Chiron teaches through the dream ways in which to accommodate woundedness, to accept that which can no longer be changed and to forgive where necessary, and thus enable healing to occur. There is often a clear lesson to be learned from dreams when this is the most potent aspect. The Chiron factor is that of the inner teacher, and makes contact with collective wisdom. Resolution of distress can often be the result of such dreams, as the dreamer makes the conscious connection between the wounded self and current aspects of his life, and gains from the wisdom that is within. Mercury–Chiron aspects are very potent; by them the dreamer can learn much about his own response patterns in waking life. The 'inner child' may speak through Mercury and that child side of the dreamer can be healed by the learning and healing that is possible through the process of dreaming.

Mercury in Aspects to the Nodes of the Moon

The nodes of the Moon in astrology are the points at which the Moon crosses the ecliptic; they represent a quest undertaken in life, that of individuation, for individuation is the quest of everyone. When Mercury aspects the nodes, there is no specific message as such, more a direction or signpost. Mercury in aspect to the north node will bring into the dream indications as to whether the person is truly in touch with his inner search – whether conscious and soul dimensions of individuation are heading in the right direction. When Mercury aspects the south node, the dream can indicate some facet of life that is irrelevant – the true quest has become obscured by material concerns. While the nodes have no capacity to motivate or to assume power within the psyche, the rational mind can decipher a sense of direction and purpose. Other aspects Mercury makes, besides the nodal contacts, will give a clearer picture of the message. The nodes represent the inner dragon or karmic path, and it is the symbolic dragon that we need to fight in order to reconnect with spiritual wholeness. The dreamer might do this consciously by having a sense of destiny, a great purpose in life that is all-consuming, a personal 'holy grail', and so the dream with Mercury–node aspects might bring some symbolic message in terms of that grail search. If the grail in conscious life is in positive tune with the process of individuation, then the message might reassure the dreamer. The karmic journey is on track, so to speak. If the conscious search is not positive, then the message might be one of division and abandonment of the quest. Aspects to planets will be more specific in their expression of the message.

3

Moon –
Illuminating Soul's Intent

It needs a very moon-like consciousness indeed . . . to talk and act in such a way that the harmonious relation of the parts to the whole is not only not disturbed but is actually enhanced. And when the ditch is too deep, a ray of moonlight smoothes it over . . .

Dr C. G. Jung

Astronomically the Moon has no light of its own, only that reflected from the Sun. Symbolically, the Moon takes in the light of the Sun, in a passive and receptive way, and reflects it back. So the Moon is a mirror, a solar collector. We have examined how, in astrology, the path of the Sun expresses the symbolism of man's conscious journey through life, and we now can see how the Moon represents the reflective, inner face of that journey. All life experience, in an outward sense, is absorbed into the inner dimension and held there, stored by the Moon's symbolic capacity to retain and contain.

Early mankind created rituals in connection with the Moon: eclipses were viewed as portents of doom, while agricultural man used – as some still do – the phases of the Moon for planting. Moon rituals were significant in the life cycles of women in particular. Ancient goddess worship represented and honoured the feminine, creative, soul principle of life in the image of the Moon, and the three main phases of the Moon are personified in the three 'faces' of the Moon goddess: virgin, mother and crone. The three principal faces are part of a process of life and death, and so the Moon's significance as part of a natural cycle of life is deeply embedded in the collective psyche.

Primitive man's identification of the potential for death, as well as for fertile life, with the Moon's image became embedded in the psychic structure of tribal and national characteristics, and so social ritual developed to honour, appease and court the favour of the Moon. For the primitive, night was the 'domain' of the goddess, a time when the goddess's capacity to create, to nurture, but also to devour was dominant – a time of fear as well as hope. Dreaming was a time when the soul left the body at the will of the Moon and travelled the spirit landscape. Appropriate rituals prepared the dreamer for the soul journey. The Moon and dreaming have always had a connection in the collective psyche but preparation for dreaming, through ritual, prayer and abandonment to the will of the spirit of night, has become a lost art in our modern times.

Our modern world has left us with remnants only of the early ceremonies and rituals that paid honour to the Moon and its soul meaning. The threefold dimension of the Moon goddess connects us to the past, the present and the future, to childhood, adulthood and the dimension of ancient wisdom. It symbolizes phases of growth and decay in psychic life. An ancient symbolism embodied in the Moon is that of the universal Mother, a receptacle for the seeds of the creative Father – a fecund source of vital new life. The Moon's glyph can be seen as a vessel into which the seeds of consciousness are poured throughout life, a womb, a source of regeneration. Purity is the youthful face of the Moon, one that is transient and defensive. Mythic virgins are cloaked with simplicity, keeping them perpetually in a childlike state, defensive and defended by the gods. Innocence is a silvery thread of illusion, but one that never completely leaves us, even though we may become cynical.

We must all mourn the loss of innocence. The most profound wound of all is the loss of childhood, for it can never be regained. Inevitably, too, we are faced with the loss of fertility as we approach the stage in life that is represented by the aged crone face of the goddess. The face of age is that which connects with our own potential death and rebirth. This aspect of the goddess is a fearsome face, yet it embodies the wisdom of time. Dreams will reflect the dreamer's inner growth phases, not necessarily in a chronological sense, but as aspects of the personality as it experiences cycles of growth, fertility and decay, and is reborn.

At bedtime, we enact a routine, which puts us in touch with our ancient roots. We spend time making up our sleeping quarters so that they are pleasant and comforting, safe and warm. Our sheets are spread on the bed; whether it is a king-sized fourposter or a mat on the floor there is a preparation process to be gone through as we prepare to enter the realm of sleep. Our ablutions are performed in much the same way as the worshipper cleansed himself before appearing before his goddess. We remove all traces of our daytime activities, abanson our persona and enter the world of sleep. Rarely, however, do we consciously realize how we are preparing for a continuation of the diurnal journey. Our preparations are blinded by our conscious thoughts and are no longer ritualistic – we have lost touch with the intrinsic meaning of preparation. At night, the day's activities, a lifetime's activities, are retranslated and embellished, and, on waking from our dreams, we are able to perceive what the unconscious makes of those daily activities. Too often, we dismiss our dreams, yet the natural and primitive curiosity that connects us to our ancestral roots remains to intrigue and fascinate. We would gain more from dreaming if we approached sleep with the same reverence that our ancestors did.

The Moon's significance, in symbolic form, is complex. It is not easy to find a core meaning for the Moon, as it represents ancient energy clothed in cultural robes that have passed through generations of experience. We need to see it not only personified in the image of the great goddess but also as an etheric space, or gestalt – the void from which all life emerged. In the image of the void, we touch on the primeval foundations of humanity and the individual. This place is the dimension of *anima*, of soul, and the lunar image contains all our personal history as well as that of our family, tribe, nation and species. We tend to view our personal past through the experiences of the ego, so memory can often be false memory, sanitized by the selectivity of conscious life. The Moon part of the personality acts as a mediator between what we think we remember and what we are really experiencing in the instinctual and feeling levels of soul. In entering the Moon's realm, we are pulled back into the subliminal self, that which is deeply submerged in the realm of the collective Moon. The polarity of the astrological Sun and Moon, as the conscious and unconscious facets of the whole self, reflects and symbolizes the main dilemma occurring in the individuation process.

Astrologically, in natal Moon potential, we experience that part of the self most subject to conditioning, because of its connection with nurturing, childhood and the family. We live lunar lives for our first two years, attached to world mother and conditioned by life in and around the cradle. During this time, unconscious response patterns are shaped, for our very survival depends, during this lunar phase of development, on world mothers, or family environmental factors. Responses become habitual, and in adult life we rarely question our emotions and feelings or attempt to change feeling behaviours. We dig more and more into old and comfortable, tried and true response patterns. The Moon self becomes a creature of habit, distanced from ancient roots and collective origins.

Clearly the Moon aspect of the self absorbs all conscious experience and is on constant alert as the experiences and relationships of conscious life act out their dramas. Each experience is relayed to the deep centre of the lunar self. The information passes across the threshold between conscious and unconscious, to be evaluated, and rearranged into feelings and responses, and melded with experience of a similar nature. It is blended, too, with the historical experience of the collective and hence images that are invoked may not be strictly personal but rather connect us to universal soul levels, just as our conscious journey connects us to our fellow travellers. Experiences are stored in a state of flux along with all the collective memories and experiences, and are only identified in the dream dimension. As our conscious environment moulds our lives, it tends to dictate, and therefore creates direct conflict with our unconscious life.

The stresses that arise out of this conflict can be highlighted in dreams by the soul's attempt to regain lost ground. The fusing of Sun and Moon, in their astrological models, is the integration of the whole. When the seeding potential of solar energy reaches fertile ground, new life emerges. This constant dynamic is worked through in dreams and the split between conscious and unconscious can be healed by observing the soul's demands for attention. The Moon is the 'beacon of awareness' in the dream chart and so is the focal point of awareness in interpreting the chart. The environment of our dreams is like new and uncharted territory, a constantly changing landscape, and the explorer requires a light to find his way. We have had our solar daylight to show the touchstones of our ego reality; now we need the lunar night light.

The Moon's passage, circling the entire zodiac in 29.4 days, is the chief significator of where the inner theatre is being acted out. Time is the chief component in determining why we dream a particular dream at a particular time. The Moon conspires with time to be in specific position to direct our attention to the play that is being enacted. It is the Moon's position by house, in the dream chart, that lights up the stage and acts as a spotlight to bring a focus on a particular area of life experience, whether conscious or unconscious. Every house has both conscious and unconscious relevance, and it is the unconscious storehouse of experience related to that house upon which the Moon shines her light – that house and the house opposite, for a light will always reflect off its opposite surface.

Conscious dimensions are available to us through the passage and cycles of the astrological Sun. In the same way, unconscious dimensions are available to us in dreams, through the astrological Moon. It connects us to the mystical womb, the beginnings of time, so that it connects to a state of being, or a locus of fertile growth. It exerts an enormous pull towards the past, so it is not surprising that issues and dilemmas we thought well dealt with can re-emerge in dreams. The Moon invokes sleep and dreaming, invites, seduces and inveigles us into the bottomless abyss, where, in passing the boundaries, we must abandon all resistance. It opens the door to the shadow dimensions of evil as well as the soul dimensions of love. Until we dream, we have no idea what we might encounter, as the images, drawn by Mercury, emerge and connect with both personal and primeval facets of self, illuminated by the Moon.

The Moon draws on the collective storehouse to create an allegorical language, for here there are no words, only imagery. Reality becomes surreal and the rational becomes irrational. The complexities of conscious life filter into soul life and are contained there, those of the present, those of the past, all contained in a vast storehouse, represented by the Moon. When working with dream charts, we find the connection between conscious and unconscious, represented by the Sun and Moon, in a process Dane Rudhyar is known to have developed – the lunation cycle.[1] Each month, starting with a new moon, a phase relationship is struck between the two luminaries. When there is an aspect between the Sun and Moon, an examination of the phase will give insight into the link between conscious and unconscious.

The following describes the quadrature phases of the Moon, which do not include Rudhyar's crescent, gibbous, disseminating and balsamic phases.

New Moon

At the new moon, we see a close blending of conscious and unconscious; a new seed of creative energy is planted and fertilized, and the opportunity for creative growth begins. In the dream chart a new-moon phase, or conjunction of Sun and Moon, will often indicate a dream that is connected to solving a dilemma that arises from a very recent predicament or situation.

Such dreams are often only the beginning of understanding. Their message is often inconclusive and is often repeated in some other form. The dream that takes place at a new moon can indicate a dream *series*, carrying a common theme. However, dreams can be dreamed out of sequence, so in recording the dreams as a series, if they appear to carry similar themes or characteristics, it is worth looking at the series and taking the new-moon dream as the starting-point of a process. The house where the conjunction between Sun and Moon takes place relates to that area of the unconscious and conscious that is experiencing new vitality. Some aspect of life is renewed, something begins, something has died as part of the cycle of living; new attitudes, new potencies can be found in the significance of the house. The dream invites and encourages us to project the new-found opportunity for freshness into consciousness, to bring some knowledge or healing out into the light so that it is integrated in conscious life. The element in which the new moon takes place is significant in highlighting the functional base for new vitality. (Elements will be explored later in this chapter.) A vivid example of a new-moon dream is that experienced by Michael. In this dream, which he calls his Santa dream, the new Moon occurs in the fourth house.

The new Moon illuminates Michael's life at a very fundamental level, because of its fourth-house position. Because it is a new Moon, the seeds of creativity are just starting to be accessible to consciousness as something new emerges from the cradle of Michael's unconscious. There is a sense of direction through supportive sextiles to Saturn and the north node, implying creative *development*, but the Moon connection will only ever illuminate, it will not direct action, so there is a sense of anticipation of the future, rather than any connection to past experiences. The Moon highlights those facets of life that are relevant to Michael's conscious journey and his activities in daily life because its most potent aspect is the conjunction with the Sun. Consciousness and unconsciousness are involved in a 'marriage' between the subjective and objective facets of his life, and there is harmony and fecundity in this blend, productive at the most creative level of Michael's psychic process.

Mercury forms a conjunction with Uranus and Neptune, is in trine to Chiron and sextile Venus and septile Pluto. The message that Mercury speaks is the ancient language of spirit, ideals and artistry through its connection to Neptune, and the 'waking dream' to transcend the ordinary, through the meaning of Uranus. Michael's mind taps into the wisdom and healing potential of Chiron and gains pleasure through the principles of Venus. Something new is emerging from the depths of Michael's creative cauldron. This dream, because the fourth house is astrologically viewed as the house ruled by the Moon, is a graphic one of new birth and accesses the unconscious in a potent way.

We might expect then that Michael's dream will impregnate Michael with the urge to be creative and may only give a hint at where that creativity lies, because at this stage creativity is only embryonic. Michael dreamed the following dream:

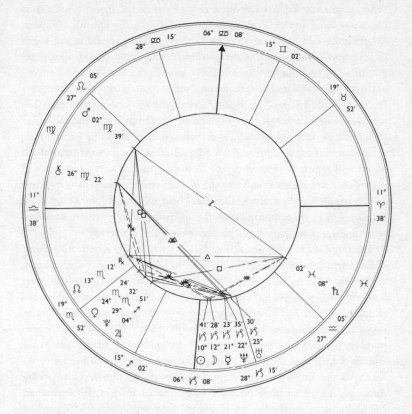

2. Michael's Santa Dream (illustrating new-moon dreaming)

'I had moved to a new house, temporary I think. It was in a town called West something, I didn't catch the rest of the name. In the house Santa Claus was sitting in a chair, murdered. I had a child in the dream, a daughter. My daughter said we must capture the killer, and as she said it, she began to turn into Santa Claus, the two bodies blending into one. I carried her upstairs – by now she was Santa Claus – and I put her in a bath. I knew I must use chemicals and electric wire to rebirth him to get to my daughter but as soon as I began, he began to change back into my daughter and recovered completely. She was covered in blood but it was the old man's blood and she was not injured. As she was cleaning herself, I began to call the police, but the number was on a liquid crystal strip at the base of the phone and kept moving from right to left, with more and more numbers, I dialled about 15 numbers and was still dialling when a young man appeared at the window with a two-headed axe. The window broke as he came through, but I used my mind power to send him back. The dream went into reverse, like rewinding a film. I awoke feeling very powerful!'

The imagery in this dream alone tells a story of new creativity. Old 'Santa Claus' might represent the demise of Michael's illusions and childish fantasy, traditions and even his own childhood, to be replaced with the 'daughter', who, after being rebirthed, cleansed herself of the blood of birthing. Mercury's connection with Neptune speaks of that illusionary quality and, by its connection with Uranus, speaks of the inspirational way in which the higher mind might understand the message. There is, because of the new Moon and its fourth-house position, an element of rebirth in some aspect of Michael's psyche. A coming of age, so to speak, at some level of psychic development, as he takes his place as parent of his ideas or brainchild. Michael is an established writer and at the time was thinking about writing another play but has only a vague idea of what he will write about.

The tone of the dream with its alchemical bath and ritual nature makes this an exciting and significant dream. Many new-moon dreams will find their 'conclusion' later, so one would not expect Michael to come to any conclusion about this dream beyond a feeling of anticipation. Later he was to have another dream, which will be examined, that clarified much of the content of this one.

The First Quarter

At the opening square there is a tension between the conscious and the unconscious, and the Moon attempts, by selecting this time to clarify some facet of the psyche, to bring matters to a head – to resolve a situation that might be 'stuck'. The first square is a point of crisis and the true meaning of the word crisis is a time for action. Dane Rudhyar explains:

... the first quarter symbolizes a crisis in relationship – an actional crisis which involves both the repudiation of what does not harmonize with the growing life and the deliberate building of new structures and faculties which will make it possible for the coming full Moon illumination to be held and assimilated. The period following the first-quarter phase is one in which obstacles must be overcome, the enmity of the old world must be met.[2]

Metamorphosis is taking place at a psychic level through dreams at this phase angle. While the dreams may be stressful, the dreamer can often experience a resolution if he is able to embody the change. Dreams at this time challenge us to break our set patterns of behaviour and attitude – to take courage in abandoning links with the past, forged through relationships, attitudes and conditioned feelings, and search for fuller awareness of our inner potential. The dream often directs us to take independent action in conscious life. This aspect highlights unresolved issues connected to family and hierarchical structures.

The dreamer is often unwilling to consciously accept that the dream indicates a critical turning-point, for as the Sun symbolically regains its power, on waking, what is expressed in the dream is often denied in the cold hard light of day. The dream connects us to the past in personal ways, so that the images and our reaction to them can tend towards the infantile. The levels of insecurity reflected in bad dreams at this time take us back to the first theme of abandonment in our conscious lives: the first time Mother let us down and the accompanying rage that was part of the experience. Small wonder that we are inclined to avoid facing the immature images of the dream. Despite a non-accepting outer attitude, a new opportunity is emerging and it may be some time before the full realization of this is integrated into consciousness. Problems that are current often have their root cause in old conditioned patterns of behaviour. It is at this time that we can examine and reconcile preconceived notions and work on the dream imagery to overcome established prejudicial stances in dealing with life and relationships.

The Full Moon

The opposition of the sun and moon creates the full moon and separates the luminaries at their greatest distance. Full moon has been traditionally viewed as the time of greatest madness and, because the Moon is 'in charge' of the unconscious realm, the unconscious becomes the source of greatest power. Solar energies have taken a back seat, and despite the apparent face-to-face nature of the full-moon phase, Moon is often dominant. Dreams with this aspect will carry themes that connect strongly to the collective unconscious as the mind swings to the extremes of the image realm and draws the ego dimension deep below the surface of our conscious reality. Thus they can be fraught with images that are challenging and seem to make no personal sense.

It is common to experience dreams of panic, fear and horror which, for the dreamer, seem to have little contact with personal dilemmas but on deeper examination most often have a very direct connection with them. Denial of the dream imagery and its message is also quite common. Dream images need to be given form and confronted, for there is something very powerful taking place, at a psychic level, in the struggle between the two representatives of individuation – the Sun and the Moon. Emotional relationships with others in conscious life and the relationship of the split parts of the self are features in dreams at this time. Facets of these dilemmas, often rooted in old behavioural patterns and responses, are brought symbolically into the light, and what is dreamed is quite often more comfortable if left in the shadows. It cannot be left in the dark, though, for the psyche selects the time to make the dreamer aware and so there is a confrontational quality in the intent of the dream. Images are carried into consciousness and need to be rationalized in active life. In consultative dialogue between dreamer and astrologer, there is the potential for resolution to a personal issue being worked out if the dreamer is encouraged to take an observer role in the dream, seeing his own dilemmas enacted and resolved by 'characters'. The full Moon might highlight aspects of life we do not want to deal with, aspects that are connected with pre-verbal and prenatal experiences that have resulted in psychic trauma. The Moon now brings suppressed feelings and images into the light. A paradox often appears in the imagery of the dream. It is expressed in an objective and rational motivation or challenge to make forward movement in conscious life, yet is based on subjective and often deeply suppressed emotions. Thinking and feeling functions are distinctly bipolar. As we wake up and return to outer life, the inner subjective imagery will chafe and needle until we take action. An example of a full-moon dream is Marie's noose dream. Note that the Moon is not *yet* full, but in the gibbous phase – however, it does polarize the first and seventh houses.

Marie dreamed, 'I woke and went into my sitting-room, because the light of the moon was too bright in my bedroom – in the dream, not in reality. As I crossed the room, which was in the dark, something touched my left cheek and I felt to see what it might be. It was a knotted rope, a noose, suspended from above, and each time I turned to avoid it, it struck me in the face. I felt something at my feet and bent to find a dead cat. I woke up and felt I had learned something in the dream although I was upset at the loss of the cat.'

The Moon is in the seventh house and is in opposition to the Sun in the first. The Moon makes a number of aspects in this chart, all of which are worth exploring, even though the dream is rather brief. There is a forming square to Saturn, a quincunx to Mercury in the second house, and trines to the conjunction of Uranus and Neptune in the fourth house. We can define, by hard aspects, that this dream is about Marie's identity, as expressed through her primary relationship, her traditional attitudes, the values imprinted on her by her family. It highlights self-defeating thought patterns and blocks, and brings her faculty for reasoning into focus.

The soft aspects bring the archetypes of idealism and change into the picture. The Moon neither motivates nor makes any statement, but simply illuminates these aspects of her life. While there is no judgement, she is confronted with her own attitudes and expectations of relationship as the Moon 'spotlights' the first house. Objectivity and subjectivity, specifically her mental outlook in the primary relationships in her life and her relationship with her inner self, are edified. The square to Saturn indicates rigidly held issues of security, of family values, and of regulations and traditions. Trines to the conjunction of Neptune and Uranus are healing and illuminate the concept that, for Marie, change in expectations of security within intimate relationships might not be so difficult as the full-moon nature of the dream would imply.

Mercury, in aspect to both Jupiter and Saturn, representatives of the mores of the social conditions that consciously and unconsciously shape

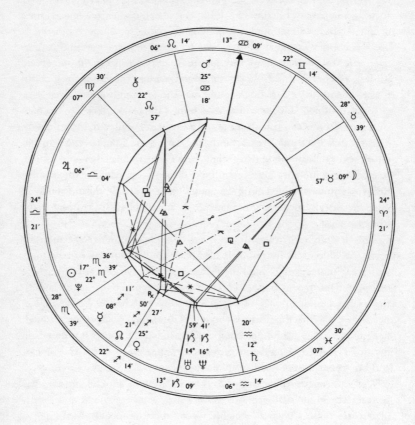

3. Marie's Noose Dream (illustrating full-moon dreaming)

our lives, 'speaks' of social, moral and ethical values, and rules of correctness as they are imprinted on Marie's psyche. There is ambivalence in the manner in which Mercury stands midway between the two planets — such mores are being reworked, questioned or transformed. The desire for growth and independent action is being affected by fixed and solid self-defeating mechanisms, rooted in the ethical and moral values taught to Marie.

This dream, then, is about a moral dilemma and a need to rethink her own role in waking life, specific to the area of relationship. The quincunx with the Moon also shows ambivalence between mind and feelings, and indicates that some intellectual stand needs to be made, that adjustments in mind-set are called for and that feelings and intuitions may be being denied in waking life. Mercury is a pivotal point which speaks in the language of the Moon, Jupiter and Saturn, all about Marie's primary relationship. It points to indecision, while the full Moon is forcing the issue in some way. Morality emerges as the significant purpose of this full-moon dream.

Marie did not like what we discovered through dialogue. She resisted understanding the dream, although I had no doubt that she did, at an intuitive level, fully understand its meaning. This is not uncommon with full-moon dreams. She contacted me a few months later, to tell me that even though she didn't, at the time, want to accept what was being shown in the dream, the dream stayed with her. At the time of the dream, Marie had been separated from her husband for about eighteen months. He kept returning for sexual gratification and his demands were becoming more bizarre and freakish. Marie had earlier decided that she would 'wait for him to come to his senses', because she believed in the commitment of marriage, for 'better or worse'. She now understood that the marriage was over and that it was only because of her built-in morality that she was still 'hanging around'!

The Last Quarter

The closing square of the Moon to the Sun will invoke dreams that are ready for integration in conscious life. The dream might show, by the house position of the Moon, what must be abandoned, accepted or integrated as part of the 'system' of living. So closing square dreams will indicate what we might need to let go of in order to transform. As with any square, there is potential tension and a conflict between the desire of the waking intellect for conscious growth and the primitive, comfort-seeking self. Dreams with this aspect connect to the social, collective, ideological and environmental themes in life, separating the adult from the child, yet highlighting the levels of innocence that remain. They will often indicate traces of naïvety at some level and such naïvety can often be at the base of the social dilemmas we face. In this phase, dreams can highlight the paradoxical nature of our consciousness, as feelings must be integrated into consciousness in a mature way. Images may highlight guilt responses and mechanisms. These are reflective dreams, so they may point the way back to the subjective roots of objective dilemmas. What cannot be changed at a conscious level will have the possibility of being changed at an unconscious level, only requiring that the dreamer reinforce inner values and accept the power of introspection. The closing square is a time for preparation for some sort of death, in order that new fertile growth can occur. The tensions that arise in dreams at this phase are often emotional – some part of the emotional self is dying, facing transformation.

Of course these are not the only aspects made between the Moon and Sun, but they do represent critical points – turning-points; in dreams they indicate exactly that, a turning-point at some level. Between each of these points are phases of unfolding when the Moon will be in other relevant aspects to the Sun. The implications of what specific aspects mean are examined in depth in Chapter 7. In the lunation cycle, all aspects created up to the full Moon are forming or waxing, and imply that something is developing or emerging. Those aspects formed after the full Moon are closing or waning aspects and imply that something is completed and is being assimilated. Between the new Moon and first quarter (square), the crescent phase, we find (using only the aspects to be used in the dream chart) that the Moon will aspect the Sun with a novile, septile, sextile and quintile. At this phase, what began at the new Moon begins to emerge, creatively, but is hesitant, so dreams will tend to carry a quality of uncertainty.

The 'Dark Phase'

As the Moon closes its cycle, it enters a phase called 'balsamic', a few days before the coming new Moon. There is a period when the Moon's light is not seen when it enters the final stages of the balsamic phase – this we call the 'dark Moon' phase, when the Moon is no longer visible from earth.

This is a time when, symbolically, the old Moon dies to be reborn as a new Moon. It invokes images of death, the grave and a fearful time when souls in ancient times were thought to be lost. Sleeping people were never disturbed in this phase, for fear the soul would not be able to return to the body. The images in dark-phase dreams dwell in the deepest reaches of the psyche, rooted in childhood and in the collective experience, and such dreams will inevitably present images that can be disquieting, yet offer the greatest opportunity for dealing with latent issues. During this time the dreamer reaches into the depths of Hades, the very bottom of the pit, or the cauldron, in which there may reside many fiends and monsters and where the ancient crone face of the moon goddess is seen. Dark-phase dreams may evoke feelings and memories long buried, even pre-verbal experiences and indeed prenatal ones. The utmost care should be taken when a dreamer reports such a dream. We may learn much about the shadow self through dreams at this time, but may also need to deal with long-buried issues.

Examining the conscious and unconscious relationship as expressed by the Sun and Moon in the dream chart, we have a picture of the connection between the inner soul self and the outer ego self, in an ever-changing evolvement, reflected in dreams. There is another factor to be taken into consideration in interpreting the dream chart and its purpose, and that is the matter of 'elements'. The Moon will change signs every two and a half days as it appears to travel the circle of the ecliptic, and in doing so, it changes from one element to the next. While these signs in the dream chart have less importance than in natal astrology, the element expressed in them is important. Elements equate to the fundamental functional 'nature' of the personality. They are the 'essence' of life – fire, earth, air and water – the primary functional ways in which we express ourselves and our life experiences. They are the source of creative and material energy.

In day-to-day life we have little real awareness of the elemental 'essence' that regulates and expresses our life experience. The connection to 'being' comes to us through the four familiar elements, so the active, the physical, the intellectual and the feeling nature is somewhat taken for granted, without the basis of those energies being examined. The Moon in the elements makes a connection to the elemental experience of being, collecting, nurturing and disseminating the energy of the element through the psyche. The four elements equate to the four 'temperaments', the functional ways in which the planetary archetypes express their principles. Intuition connects to the fire element and is active, spirited and initiating. The sensate connects to the earth element, and its temperament is practical, pragmatic and stable. That of feeling is emotional, perceptive and reflective, and it correlates with water. Thinking, intellect, logic and rationale correlates with the element air. In Marie's dream, the Moon is in the earth element, represented by the sign Taurus, and her dream did indeed highlight issues connected to the worldly and physical elements of her marriage.

THE MOON IN THE ELEMENTS

The Moon in Earth

We experience earth as a sense of connectedness, of relatedness with others and with the paradigms that unconsciously define our position in the wider collective. The physical senses give information to the psyche of the perceived realities and structural forms of how the world and the individual's place in it function.

Earth 'grounds' the self and addresses the practical issues that connect to the physical body, to health and well-being, to encapsulated security, or the comfort zone. Earth holds and gives form to the spirit of self in the physical dimension. It is the organic structural being; it is enduring, takes no risks, ponders over dilemmas, resists change and takes comfort in sameness. When the moon is in this element, the dream purpose is linked to the 'realities' of structured life and the latent comfort that structure brings. It brings to light the aspects of self that may be in need of reworking – issues that have become stagnant or disjointed, suffocating from misuse – to be broken down and re-formed into a more workable structure. It also brings into the light the working and solid, reliable, habitual parts of self and the inner capacity to ride out the storm, to endure hardship and to be patient and resilient.

Dreams with an earth Moon will often associate with current issues and aspects of the past that provide comfort, even those that are painful. Dilemmas that emerge in dreams are often rooted deeply in habit and may be in need of a quite considerable change of attitude. There is often strong resistance to the message of the dream, which, while it is expressed in familiar images, is slightly distorted. Dreams will sometimes have a 'setting' that is close to or resembles the dreamer's own physical environment, and the more this environment is changed in the inner landscape, the more there seems to be a call for change at a basic and practical level. It offers scope to determine what needs to be discarded, what is outworn and no longer workable, and what needs to be done. Dreams express the breaking up of components of whole-life experience and familiarities so that they can be reconstructed and re-formed in a similar manner, but with a modified relationship with life. The dream with an earth Moon can often be the first inkling of impending changes in the dreamer's world and environmental experience — as though the earth is beginning to rumble and grumble with a potential volcanic outburst.

The Moon in Air

Air is beyond the scope of the physical; it transcends the prosaic and is not limited by boundaries, or even direction. Life and all life activities, conscious or unconscious, seem to emanate in some way from an idea, a concept of universal order and wisdom, a universal mind. The relationship with the self through the air element is speculative; it is the vast energy of the abstract, of imagination and perception through patterns and theory. It enables the psychic self to detach from worldly concerns and from emotional pain, and to take no action other than to explore potentialities.

In the dream chart, when the Moon is in air it is connected to the intellectual capacity of the self, as well as accessing and drawing from the universal mind. Rational thought, balance between possible and impossible, and the cosmic meaning behind life are all available to the dreamer. Air transcends the boundaries of time and so the dream might be related to the individual's past, present and future. It is through air-moon dreaming that the clairvoyant dream can be experienced. The Moon's placement in air enables the dreamer to lift the mind to a higher level of cosmic connectedness and stand 'outside' conscious life to survey that life from an objective viewpoint, to separate selfish interests and see order.

The dream purpose is linked to the intellectual expression of conscious life and if that conscious life is in disarray, to view it and find logical solutions to dilemmas. The air Moon lights the unconscious mind with the new ways of thinking, brings to light the mind-set, and touches the force and power of the mind to analyse, pre-empt, and cope with change. The dreamer can review life experiences and 'rewrite the script' of stagnant thought patterns, objectifying those matters from the past that may have been instrumental in creating an unimaginative approach to conscious life. Air-moon dreams often have a 'setting' that is exotic and beyond the dreamer's own environment, or may have no structured form or landscape. The dreamer will do things in his dream which range from the sublime to the ridiculous. They often come in a series, when the dreamer explores his own potential in an abstracted 'what if' way, and their value is in stimulating and feeding the psyche with an infusion of possibilities. The air-moon function is through mental channels, giving the dreamer the opportunity to reconsider his options.

The Moon in Fire

Fire captures the vital and combustible spirit of the self as expressed in conscious life. There is a spontaneous flow of dynamic energy that is wilful and intentional. It can come in a steady stream or in a volcanic rush that imbues the individual with self-motivating force. It brings hope, uncompromising and often naïve. This is expressed in an optimistic and incautious faith in self and will impel the individual to constant movement and action.

In the dream chart, when the Moon is in fire, it is drawing on that element to highlight the capacity of the dreamer to initiate, to use the power of will; he is motivated to take action and aim for victory over the mundane. The dream purpose links to the desire for experience, for adventure and for creative endeavour, illuminating the more conscious, ego experience of current events and phases that empowers the expression of animus, or the masculine principle of action. It brings to light ethical and religious ideals, passions and opportunities that generate creativity and the seeding of new conscious life. It touches the animating and self-asserting forces that revitalize life with courage and strength. It initiates enterprise and challenge and the capacity to fight with the inner and outer demons in a courageous and heroic way, often showing the force that is behind current dilemmas. It reaches the intuitive self and reawakens what is stifled by material concerns. Moon dreams in fire awaken faith in self and the dreamer's capacity to decide on action. Such dreams are in effect a call to arms, to take the initiative in some way, and dreamers often express a sense of purpose after such a dream. An intuitive revelation may occur, and old anger and rage may be released. Because we experience fire as a conscious, initiating, active experience this position indicates that the dream purpose is to act consciously.

The Moon in Water

The water element connects with all that is mystical, not understood by any other means than feelings. Emotions, illusions, nurturing principles, needs, pain and ecstasy are all experienced through this element. Yet we are unable to grasp its meaning fully by rational means, only by symbolic and allegorical means. Water is the dream dimension, the state in which all the feeling components of self are accessed through the Moon's placement in the dream chart and reintroduced to the dreamer. Feelings and emotions that may have been denied, choked or misinterpreted by the conscious mind are evoked for transformation. Conscious life has many intangible experiences, subtleties that in some way influence without being apparent. Coincidences, or synchronistic events, are often only seen with hindsight and we then wish we could have recognized the signals at the time.

We experience the water element as mystical, subtle and reflective, and the Moon here enables the dreamer to tune into the deeper parts of psychic experience. It connects to the sense impressions left by experiences and relationships, it stimulates the empathic nature and tunes in the victimized and martyred experience of the dreamer. Resentment of sacrifices made in the past has enormous power to control and manipulate lives negatively, if it is retained, and not released through forgiveness and healing.

Dreams with a water Moon are notable for their emotional nature: the impressions and images are often indescribable and difficult to articulate. The demons of the 'bad' dream threaten by their ability to shape shift. The Moon brings to light hidden fear and terrors, but also the capacity for love. Dreams may seem to destroy and devour aspects of the emotional self but the dreamer returns to consciousness imbued with revitalized feelings reborn out of the inertia or the paralysis of frozen emotions. Such dreams are often better understood through their capacity to renew feelings, rather than through being intellectualized, and they are marked by a commentary on feelings as the dreamer tells the story. They may be inconclusive, yet powerful in their capacity to transform. This can be a painful process. At an emotional level, suppressed rage is often more accessible and we may attempt to intellectualize forgiveness. Habitual and conditioned emotional sensors are reworked and new ways of experiencing feelings can emerge. Meeting dimensions of one's own soul in water dreams can be confronting, revealing and reassuring, and lead to greater acceptance of what cannot be changed from the past. The experience can bring both despair and joy. Kelly's blob dream, with a water Moon, examined on pp. 19–22, brought to light many conditioned emotional sensors and resulted in an acceptance of aspects of her life that were still painful.

Added information is given through the Moon's aspects to planets in the chart. The Moon's principal function in the chart is to light up an area of house experience that is in need of attention. By aspecting other planets, the principles of those planets are brought into view and are able to make a contribution to the imagery of the dream. The Moon makes no direct statement but illuminates and 'involves' those planets in the dream, according to their meaning.

If the Moon opposes a planet it brings that planet into very high focus, and the meaning embedded in the planet can often be interpreted as the main purpose behind the dream. Those that are square are involved, light is shed, obliquely, and those planets' principles may be interpreted as 'issues' connected in some way with the purpose of the dream. The Moon is throwing light on to some difficult aspects of the principles embodied in the planet's meaning. Those in soft aspect are passively involved and may not be connected to an 'issue' but highlight the more positive principles of that planet. Synthesizing the Moon's element with its connection by aspect to other planets will indicate the functional basis of the dream purpose. Examination of its connection to other planets and sensitive points, and of its house position, shows the intent of the dream – what is being shown to the dreamer.

Viewing the dream as a drama, some players play potent roles while others play bit parts, supporting the main characters. If we can imagine the Moon as the essential light of the stage, floodlight and spotlight, with Mercury as writer and narrator, we can now explore the symbolic meaning of the other planets.

4

The Inner Planets –
Meeting Facets of Self

The greatest act of faith that a man can perform is the act we perform each night. We abandon our identity, we turn our soul and body into chaos and old night.

G. K. Chesterton

THE 'PERSONAL' PLANETS

Those planets which orbit within sight of the Sun are symbolically those that are closest to consciousness. Following on from the premise that the Sun represents the central identity, it follows that those in close proximity will be distinguished by awareness. As each planet orbits further from this central core, they approach the realm of the collective, those meanings that are less personal and are more common to everyone. The planets we call 'personal' are the Sun, Moon, Mercury, Venus and Mars; the Moon and Mercury have already been discussed, in Chapters 2 and 3.

The Sun

Conscious activities, experiences and relationships all give parameters within which we identify living existence. Recognition of the familiar affords us comfort and sustenance for conscious living. Katharine Merlin quotes Esther Harding: 'The ego, in the sense in which the word is used in analytical psychology, represents the centre of consciousness of the adult personality, the focal point of all we have known or experienced in life that has remained conscious to us. This focus of consciousness gradually becomes organized from its first nebulous beginnings till at adolescence a recognizable and relatively stable personality emerges.'[1]

Astrologers often connect the Sun with the father in the formative years of the ego, the implication being that through the father, or some other masculine role model's activities, much of the capacity to identify with external life is modelled. There is a deeper, more collective implication though, as the child is born with a 'hero figure' embedded in the psyche. To the immature personality, someone outside of the self who represents a centralizing figure becomes the manifestation of this inner hero. At some time during the formative years, the growing child separates his own sense of self and begins to recognize himself by his own 'I' identity.

He is left, however, with the archetypal 'hero model', which has been shaped to some extent by his worldly role model and is open to further shaping and development through his own experiences. He attaches the 'I' to his own daily experiences and relationships, and hence they shape his conscious life. Clearly, the Sun represents the 'I' in the horoscope. We awake and warm to its physical heat, light and life-giving energies; we feel uplifted by its presence, often feeling down on dull days. We know we are alive and vital because, on waking, we see the sunlight and make a connection between its light and our awareness and self-consciousness.

The Sun symbol represents the individual's life cycle and he identifies with it in the passage of the physical sun from day to day, year to year. Equinoxes and solstices are the turning-points by which the world experiences seasons of growth and decay. We experience these turning-points as they mark the personal seasons by which we live and grow in consciousness.

The sun lights the day and we follow its path in our daily activities, regulating our day by its passage across the ecliptic and then settling down to anticipate sleep as it sets. Our bodies and minds are in tune with its vital energy. Thus we identify the sun's reality with our own reality. The vital energy that brings life to the planet symbolizes the life of the psyche, but it tends to represent only the waking part of the journey through life. True individuation must integrate these principles of active and material paradigms with the unconscious side of the self, since we experience the unconscious in equal proportions.

As we awake from sleep and note that the sun has risen again, we return to material realities, setting aside the dreams of the night as sunlight and consciousness bring us into the world of the physical. In worldly life, we measure ourselves by the rewards we receive, by the accolades and applause that litter our journeys, so it is small wonder that we tend to identify wholeness and joy with the waking symbol – the Sun. In a positive way, this allows the healthy ego to value material life, to gain from and be rewarded by life through good relationships and joyous activities. Valuing conscious life is as essential to our well-being and wholeness as is valuing the unconscious. Using the insight and wisdom that come from dreaming to enhance and improve that conscious life is an opportunity that is available to all.

So, the Sun is a vital symbol of consciousness by which we identify ourselves as individual human beings. Psychologically, it separates us from the unconscious and we sense the separation and instinctively crave a state of true wholeness. Those who deny or suppress that instinct identify entirely with consciousness, and they will at some time be compelled to review the paradigms by which they live and to examine the possibility of a more meaningful existence, acknowledging the inner self.

The metaphorical 'hero's journey' identifies the urge in humanity to search for an ideal, a holy grail that will reconnect the differentiated parts of the whole. At its most meaningful that grail quest is the instinctive search for individuated self and psychic peace. To seek to experience wholeness is a deeply entrenched instinct in human nature. Our lives are a quest or journey that embodies the search to reconnect ego with soul and so find true identity. The myth of the quest embodies a profound truth and, as the symbol of the hero self, the Sun is central to the quest. Being conscious of the 'I' self as our centre of being is analogous to the position of the sun at the centre of the solar system.

Bruno Huber says, 'The Sun enables us to take up our very own stand in life from which to observe the world, to assess it and evaluate it. But everything in life, every object and situation, will be seen in relation to ourselves, and will be incorporated into our own value system. Naturally, because of our own limited capabilities, our judgement is bound to be subjective. The Sun, our central Ego, is chiefly interested in things which concern us personally, which enhance our standing and potential.'[2] I would add to 'our limited capabilities' that we limit ourselves only by our *conscious* capabilities. In dreams and in the unconscious landscape, the Sun represents the *unlimited sleeping* ego, no longer attached to conscious activities and motivations.

Psychologically the Sun represents our sense of personal mastery over life, our conscious confidence, enterprise and generative power. The Sun also represents the physical body, our capacity to sustain creative and vital life, the urge to create, to leave a worldly legacy through original endeavours and to procreate through the production of children.

Dreams where the Sun is predominant might refer to the body's health, or to the desire to create in some way, either through children or through projects that give a sense of pride or success — an identification of the dreamer as a creator. Similarly, in dreams that connect to childhood, or to deeply embedded childhood experiences, the Sun might represent the actual father, or some other masculine role model. The creative lessons imprinted on the personality by such a role model might also arise in the dream. Examination of the connection of the Sun and Moon in the lunation process should make it apparent that, whatever the dream message, it has something to do with the conscious identity, life activities, the body and the creative urges of the individual.

The Sun will be 'speaking' about identifiable conscious activities, the 'I' of waking life. Michael's Santa dream, on p. 42, illustrates the Sun as the central theme of the dream. In that dream, we saw that there was a seeding of new creative beginnings, beginnings which Michael was able to incorporate into his conscious life, when, later, he began to write a play. Marie, too, through her noose dream (p. 45), was to take up the challenge to her identity, change her name and begin a new life as a single person.

Venus

This planet is close to earth and so connects symbolically with the 'reality' of our lives. It is also close to the Sun, the symbol of identity, and is 'personal' in this respect. The principles embodied in this planet are those of harmony, equilibrium and relationship. Venus also represents the capacity to measure, instinctively, the relative worth of opposites involved in any exchange. Psychologically, it enables the individual to strike a balance between the speculative potentialities demonstrated in the desire nature of the symbolic Sun and the material probabilities represented by the Earth. We unconsciously evaluate all constituents of life – work must balance with leisure, effort with reward, affection given with affection received.

Venus is our capacity for exchange. We measure satisfaction in giving to others against the response of the recipient; physical well-being against health, wealth and tranquillity of mind; times of contentment against times of strife. Love is pivotal between what we give and what we receive. Venus is the part of the personality that maintains, or urges us to achieve, a balance between opposing or differentiated facets of life. We are born with an instinctive awareness of being separated, an awareness that is pivotal in the process of individuation. Venus is perhaps that part of the self most keenly aware of this division and we spend much of our conscious life in searching for some other person to make us feel complete. The outer partner must cope with fulfilling this role in consciousness, but it is the search for the inner partner which constitutes the harmonious relationship of parts to whole. We cannot relate with the inner Venus self without some reflective confirmation from outer relationships, and conversely we cannot relate to outer relationships without some awareness of the inner Venus. We cannot love ourselves completely without some love received from others, nor can we love others if we don't love ourselves. Venus' essential meaning is in the marriage between these opposites and in the effort to create a sense of unity.

Intellectually, Venus embodies unconditional appraisal, impartiality and the ability to make sound value judgements, to dispense justice with compassionate detachment. At a feeling level, it is empathetic with others, passive, sensual and desirous of giving and receiving pleasure. Emotionally, it is loving, sharing, affectionate and devoted. It builds an intuitive value structure in the psyche, enabling the individual to create his own set of values, which may sometimes be different to those taught by society and family.

Venus embodies harmony, the pleasure principle, the desire for unity and accord. With Venus we clarify, refine and balance ego intent with sound value judgement. Venus brings sweetness into conscious life and creates equilibrium. It attracts others to us, in attachment and concord. It brings contentment of soul, appreciation of the delights of an uncomplicated life. Its essence is love of others, love of self. When Venus formulates positively, self esteem is high and inner serenity is the reward. There is stability and support from relationships. It empowers individuals to cherish what is gratifying in their lives, and enables interaction between soul and ego to be a pleasurable, harmonious and individuating experience. The heart is glad and one appreciates the sense of being loved and valued and being able to love and value. Harmony is an aesthetic principle, and so Venus correlates with the ability to enjoy harmony in colour, shape and form, sound, sight, texture, taste and smell. It enables one to benefit from material and commercial, sexual, sociable and pleasurable activities, to feel contented and at one with self. There is no contentment or unity if one ignores the passive side of the self in the search for achievement, applause and accolades. People become indiscriminate in their daily lives when they pay scant attention to Venus, and so become dysfunctional – desire replaces love, ego denies the intrinsic benefits of receptivity – because of misplaced beliefs in a draconian path to achievement.

We become greedy as the Venus part of the self seeks compulsively to satisfy the senses. We demand attention and become manipulative. Anyone can convince themselves that being rich, admired, beautiful or sexually compelling is what pleases most and gives us a joyful life — that a life filled with pleasure is happiness. Yet there is inner discontent in trying to become more admirable, richer, more beautiful or compelling — life without love at its core looks no further than superficial activities and relationships. In desiring to convince ourselves that we are happy, we end up either desiring control and domination or being controlled and dominated.

Venus allows us to select and use the building blocks of personal and collective values — to evaluate them and maintain them via natural measures or laws that testify to peace, morality and justice, harmony and creativity. It enables us to use such measures in personal practice. We see the many faces of Venus in dreams that attempt to compensate for unfairness and discontent in conscious life.

When Venus is prominent in the dream chart it is because the psyche seeks to redress some facets in life that are out of proportion. There is something restorative whenever Venus appears as the dominant planet — even if the aspects are hard aspects. There is nothing hard about Venus; the dreams may become more explicit, the message more purposeful or defined, but there is healing and rebalancing. The dream imagery may address relationships, truths, or legal or material considerations, weigh them in the balance and indicate an answer. There can be a healing of painful relationships in conscious life through a better relationship with self, and the dream will often gently point out ways to achieve this.

Sexuality is a feature of Venus dreams — the dreamer experiences his capacity for physical love in dreams that transcend sexual inhibitions, or highlight needs, often in an enjoyable and satisfying dream! Venus is often found in a supportive aspect with other more dominant aspects and the astrologer should take care not to overlook the healing that comes with the Venus connection.

Mars

Mars symbolizes willpower and the instinct for survival. To survive and to take command requires a measure of forcefulness. We rarely appreciate aggression when we see it acted out, yet we are all capable of being combative, either in defence of, or in pursuit of, something that is important to us. While we are able to accept that we are capable of assault and offence, we rarely admit it! We *do* appreciate assertion, contrasting it with aggression, for it implies resilience, forthright action with passion and determination in the face of opposition. Aggression and assertion – the words connect to the same symbolic source, only we understand them in very different ways. Mars embodies both faces and it is essential in worldly activity, manifesting as the drive and energy to achieve; in being virile; in being able to create momentum and be competitive in a competitive environment.

In the struggle towards integration and whole relationship through individuation, we need to incorporate Mars' value and actuate it in healthy ways. Mars, symbolic of fighting spirit, is either creative or destructive. We tend to experience the Mars side of the personality more often in conscious activity, when we are more aware of action and in charge of the mechanisms that allow us to battle through life's myriad experiences.

The healthy ego directs and uses Mars as an agency to achieve goals, and controls it through recognizing the primitive instinct for survival in unknown territory. It is the Mars principle of activity that motivates and energizes. Without the motivation of Mars, there could be no movement, no achievement. Without an active and productive conscious life, we cannot appreciate soul. Positively, Mars enables us to defend those values that the individuated self holds dear, to strive for what will create a worthwhile daily life and to guard and protect committed relationships, focused goals and a healthy sense of unity. In conscious life, using the motivation principle of Mars, we may take up arms to defend the underdog with honour and dignity. Without Mars we could not right wrongs or take action against evil, nor be decisive in the face of dilemmas.

Mars enables us to cut to the heart of problems, with precision and forthright action. It imbues us with the spirited desire to wake each day with a sense of purpose and gives us the vital force with which to achieve that purpose. It sends the life blood coursing through our veins and inspires us with courage and self-confidence. A well-used and recognized Mars is essential to wholeness. Having a sense of identity and being able to express that identity consciously depends on the ability to energize, mobilize and express the self. The mobility propels the healthy ego towards individuation.

Mars also represents the fury, fears and phobias, brutality, coarseness, brashness, anger and foolhardiness, which is rooted in the shadow aspect of self. It can promote a surfeit of activity and conflict as a way of life. Through it we litter life with the dead bodies of past battles and are scarred by constant warring and defensive attitudes. When defence becomes aggression for the sake of the kill, when hot blood turns to blood lust and we use Mars energy to trample the underdog in the race to be top dog, then Mars is operating from the shadow side of the personality. People become savage, and Mars takes over control of the 'I' – separated from purpose, hell-bent on conquest for its own sake.

A suppressed or unrecognized Mars is dangerous. Lacking true purpose, the person is fearful, timid and unable to defend himself. He becomes inert, submissive and resigned to failure in his life – there is no seeking, no robust participation in life, and all the potency of Mars is trapped in the shadow, to simmer and seethe with resentment and unexpressed rage.

Life can be challenging, but Mars gives us the capacity to take on feats of clearing and cleansing, and to use our assertive skills with discrimination. Each time we must face enormous odds with courage and determination, or perform some difficult task, we have to make a conscious choice to either face it head on or to ignore it. When Mars is the dominant planet in the dream chart, we see some aspect of self that is on constant alert, so if we have ignored challenges in worldly life, or been denied the right to be self-assertive, challenges often return to provoke us in dreams. Dreamers may find Mars encourages them to action in some aspect of life; they may find this capacity exists in the personal shadow and, previously unexpressed, is free of the constraints of conditional life, and can be activated in dreaming in a potent way.

Mars in dreams acts like a surgeon in the healing process. It is rarely subtle. It can excise and release the poisons that have settled into the shadow and invoke action and decision to manifest something worthwhile in consciousness. Mars in dreams is often fighting demons and indicates ways to fight those that are part of waking life. It comes into action whenever the delicate balance of wholeness is threatened, motivated by its archetypal partner Venus. It is prominent in the following dream, dreamed by Gloria, which she titled 'Arab dream'.

Both the Moon and Mercury are opposing Mars. When Mercury and the Moon are both in aspect to the principal planet of the dream chart there is a very palpable message; when in a mutual aspect to that planet, the message is even more explicit. The self-determining, assertive side of Gloria's personality is demanding a voice. Something requires confrontation – now – because the opposition has brought some matter to a head. The ninth-house position of Mars implies that Gloria is ready to explore and widen her scope of activities. The fact that Mars is singleton, retrograde, also implies her hidden adventurousness.

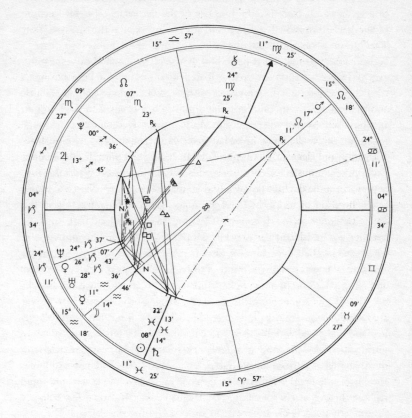

4. Gloria's Arab Dream (illustrating Mars potency)

The Moon in air connects to the intellectual, rational and objective side of life, so we might refine the purpose of the dream to a cerebral matter, rather than an emotional problem, and this is reinforced by the Mars position. The Moon is on the cusp of the second and third houses so there is conspicuous overspill of light into both houses. The second house is significant in material terms, connecting to self-worth matters; to the dreamer's capacity to acquire and preserve material; her resourcefulness and capabilities, and the value she puts on them; physical well-being; sexuality and money. It is representative of the physical body, its responsiveness to love through touch and expression of being valuable to others. The third house represents her education; the way she thinks; learned skills and ethics; her immediate environment and the effect of her environmental situation on her ability to be mobile, verbalize her thoughts and convey her value structure to others.

She dreamed, 'I was in bed with John [husband] and dreamed that I was dreaming about my car – a sort of dream within a dream. I woke up – in the dream – and heard the car start up, but I was still dreaming. I tried to wake John but he was pretending he couldn't wake up. The dog was barking and someone was moving around in the house. The dog raced up the hall and jumped on the bed and licked John's face, but he still wouldn't wake up. Then I saw someone in the doorway, looking around the door. It was a young Arab or Turk. I desperately tried to wake John, but he physically held me in the bed with his legs, so I could neither keep trying to wake him nor do anything about the intruder. I heard the sound of eastern-style rock music, tinny, as if from an old radio. I closed my eyes and saw egg lifters forming a spiral pattern. Then I really woke up and for a few seconds could still see the egg lifters spiralling towards the ceiling. It took a few minutes to decide if I was really awake, or in another layer of the dream.'

The dream imagery highlights feelings of impotence and translates into some 'foreign' intrusion in her life at the time. Gloria is a teacher, who works at a tertiary institution. At the time of the dream, she had experienced many upsets both in her personal life and in her working life. As the income earner in the family at the time of the dream, she was putting up with the unsatisfactory nature of her working life for the sake of earning money, as her husband had recently lost his job through ill-health.

In dialogue with Gloria, it emerged that the teaching she was doing was well below her capacities as a teacher; she felt forced to teach subjects that were not her forte and preparations for the lessons were intruding on her domestic and leisure time. She expressed her frustration with the job and her longing to find a new direction, or affect the classes in a creative way, but she was held back by the need to earn a living and so not rock the boat. She enjoyed teaching in a general sense. Gloria had been hesitant to discuss her problem with anyone at work until the dream brought awareness of her own suppressed anger – an anger directed both towards her job and towards her financial situation. She felt her husband was not pulling his weight and could do more towards improving their financial situation. None of these matters had been addressed because she was afraid that she would become over-emotional and lose control. She sympathized with her husband, whose sight was failing, but at the same time resented what she perceived as his casual attitude. Because her tenure at work was on a temporary basis and she hoped to make it permanent, she hesitated to deal with her frustration for fear of losing the promise of future employment.

Following the dream, Gloria decided she should take action, and was able to express her dissatisfaction to her employers, in a contained and rational way, eventually obtaining a more favourable position that enabled her to teach more creatively and earn more money. She also discussed matters with her husband and discovered that he had been trying to negotiate a pension that would not be reduced by the money she earned.

This dream illustrates the power of retrograde Mars to motivate suppressed action and decisiveness. The dream within a dream is a phenomenon that points to long stifled 'shadow motifs' and from this encounter with the suppressed Mars, Gloria learned that she needs to learn techniques for expressing all her needs more assertively. She admits having an 'anger' problem, in that she is not able to express aggression fruitfully without becoming over-emotional. She is an extremely intelligent person who has never felt satisfied that she has fully explored her intellectual capacities. The dilemma between the need to earn a living and the desire to grow intellectually has been a long struggle and, in becoming aware of this, Gloria is taking steps to make changes by expressing her ambitions in a more fruitful way. The symbolic eggs are on the move!

THE 'SOCIAL' PLANETS

The planets we have examined up to now are those that orbit close to the earth's orbit and so, astrologically, transit close to the central Sun. Because of the connection with the Sun as the central 'I' and the earth as the representative of worldly reality, we deem them 'personal planets', because we are aware of their meanings in our daily activities. The planets Jupiter and Saturn, orbit more distantly and so symbolize activity of a less personal and more socially oriented kind: They connect to those aspects of the self that relate to something outside personal experience in the search for meaning – to the collective cultural mores, laws and religions that shape social life, make one civilized and connect the individual to a 'place' in the collective environment.

Jupiter

This planet represents and expresses that within us which develops a higher purpose, so that life has meaning and relevance. Without Jupiter, life would be aimless, devoid of colour, symbolism, direction, growth or sense. Jupiter correlates with the ability to formulate a philosophy for living. Through the archetype of Jupiter we connect both to the underlying drive for power and victory over the profane and to the search for meaningful and uplifting activities that transport the self to a higher level of experience. Jupiter also represents having faith in life and in oneself. That faith translates in worldly life to moral principles, religious theorems and laws, social mores and cerebral justifications. Jupiter motivates the individual to adopt or create a personal philosophy, but also puts him in touch with a broader, more socially embodying philosophy, in tune with, or at odds with, growing personal paradigms. It acts at times like a moral arbiter, taking the prevailing social conditions and judging their fit with the inner philosophy.

It is a psychic urge to keep improving life with an infusion of joyous spirit, to rise above the irreverent and make it sacred. Positively Jupiter is that side of human nature that is benevolent and altruistic. When conscious of its positive power, one may feel close to that which we may call the higher source, or an innate sense of 'godliness'. Jupiter enables joyous appreciation of all that life offers and gives an appreciation of that which has no material value. It breathes spirituality into the psyche and encourages us to look to the universe and find meaning, truth and a personal ideal. Jupiter advocates an 'upward' movement that links the personal realm with the supernatural or spiritual realm. It can tend to inflation and either distance the ego from the introspective nature of soul, or make life a 'ride with the gods', blessed with true soul connections. Without Jupiter our lives are flat, two-dimensional and stagnant – we are spiritually stranded. Jupiter is like a bridge connecting worldly reality with the spiritual possibilities and the potential for growth that brings joy. Being involved in a spiritual belief system, and connecting the principles of truth, honour and honesty, are positive attributes contributed by Jupiter. One may seek these possibilities through belief and faith in religious doctrines or through traditional social and environmental paradigms. The truth in Jupiter is to grow through and expand those ideologies and find purpose and meaning. To do so takes courage and faith in one's own self. Howard Sasportas puts it thus: 'Jupiter ... is ... the sense that life is not just a collection of random events, but has meaning and purposeful intention. When our faith in life begins to falter, it is by looking to Jupiter's domain that we may gain inspiration to travel on.'[3]

Jupiter also represents humour, enjoyment and celebration of life, while reminding us that there is a price to pay for indulgence. This might occur in a physical way, and health suffers. Warning signals about health can be a feature of Jupiter dreams. When we neglect the celebratory side of life, it becomes grim, laden and worrisome; then Jupiter can appear in dreams that poke fun at our attitudes. Images appear that are humorous, and serve to remind us that we do not have to be victims of outer circumstances.

To illustrate this I recall a dream I had at a time when life seemed just that — depressing, miserable and pointless. I was feeling sorry for myself, forgetting to sing the 'hymn' to life; I was repeating an endless 'dirge' of parental responsibility, boredom, work and grinding routine. In the dream, I walked through a large garden accompanied by a splendid lion, two mangy cats, a hippopotamus and a cow. I was berating them loudly for not keeping the garden tidy and for urinating in inappropriate places, and I complained as I picked up discarded clothing. We all went into a house, where I began to prepare breakfast, sighing at the unfairness of it all, when a snow-white, elongated, rather fragile duck waddled in saying, 'Look at me, I'm a clever boy,' and proceeded to demonstrate how to urinate through a piece of hose, outside the door. This skinny little fellow was so comical I woke laughing and the whole mood changed, not only for me but for those around me!

Jupiter means expanding all levels of experience, body, mind, soul and spirit, and becoming a better or more fulfilled person. Jupiter can, however, blow out to such proportions that it dominates the individual and results in excess and over-confidence. The personality becomes contradictory, despotic and tyrannical, inflated by personal ideologies. When outer attitudes imply one is invincible and irreplaceable, then soul sends warning signals through

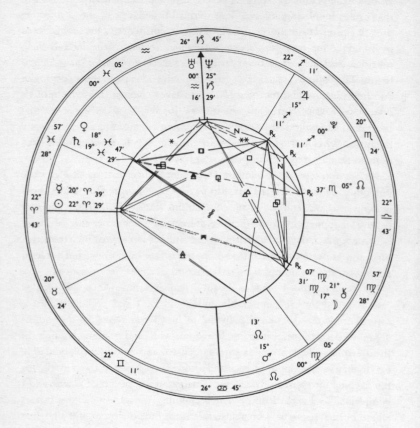

5. My Duck Dream (illustrating Jupiter potency)

dreams which illustrate the need to reconnect with a sense of humility as a requisite to wholeness.

Personal virtue is not always compatible with worldly laws and moral ethics. While Jupiter connects to the same natural laws and justice as Venus, we often find ourselves at odds with those social conditions in which we live on a day-to-day basis. Through Jupiter in the dream chart we can isolate the conditional social expectations that have been a part of our growth patterns since birth, and the dream might represent the opportunity to grow beyond such conditions. Jupiter's laws attempt to transcend time and space boundaries, and the positive message in dreams can often illustrate potential beyond waking imagination and enable the individual to transcend those boundaries in conscious activity. Kelly's blob dream on p. 20 showed, through a quincunx (adjustment) aspect between Mercury and Jupiter, how worldly laws and religious dogmas influenced her psyche and how her own natural law and ethics needed to be reclaimed. Worldly experience, through a dictatorial parent and religious dogma, had been a stagnating experience for Kelly in childhood, and through the dream she could discover her own truths and make progress in life.

Saturn

Saturn represents the capacity to structure and refine, to create boundaries and standards. In life, there are rules, regulations and taboos that serve to establish the individual within the framework of a group. This planet is the last of the 'visible' planets, the one that represents the limits of what we can perceive in the universe and so, symbolically, represents the limits of personal and social experience – the bridge to the gestalt of the outer or transpersonal planets. Such limits and boundaries are what keep one 'civilized' and able to live in groups with respect for others and appropriate values. Saturn, by balancing and complementing Jupiter, gives a framework for expansion, helps control inflationary tendencies. Life can be steady, refined and deferential, learning from the experience of past generations.

The positive face of Saturn enables one to take responsibility, be self-assured, supported by a sense of order, tranquillity and steadiness in life. Tradition, family hierarchies and collective truisms underpin forward progress. Saturn teaches respect for the rights of self and others, teaches, supports, disciplines and allows young individuals to grow in a self-regulated, steady fashion towards maturity, with respect and honour paid to the standards and values of their society.

In outer life, when we experience negative Saturn, the conventional boundaries exceed fundamental, simple guidelines for living, and become confining and grim. Making progress is a journey fraught with barriers, stumbling-blocks and experiences that seem to defeat any steps we take. Saturn is the archetype of habitual and repeated patterns, of inherited modes of behaviour, taboos and traditions experienced in a collective environment, handed down through generations and so accepted as fate, seemingly pre-ordained in our genetic coding.

Natal astrology shows a predisposition, through the Saturn model, for individuals either to feel 'doomed' or to have a positive sense of destiny. In other words, some people experience Saturn in an inherently negative way and others in a positive way. When very young, we accept without question those aspects of environment and relationships that regulate and control the way we live. Experiences of a Saturn nature, coming to us at the hands of others and of society at large, emanate from the tribe or family of which we are a part. The rules and prohibitions by which we live are enormously powerful, and the negative face of this is exploitative, constraining and cruel, denying creative endeavour. Saturn is that part of the self that responds to patterning, imprinted social behaviours, unconscious hierarchical character-istics and patterns that are reinforced in childhood.

If such conditions are extreme in a negative way, psychic blows are often a continuum of inherited pains borne by those who inflict the pain. Breaking the cycle is nearly impossible – guilt, fear and habitual blame-taking responses ride the personality and seem to pass from generation to generation. Rigidity, cruelty, terror, paralysis in one form or another, often in the guise of family and social structuring actuated early in life, have become a part of an unconscious response mechanism. Many young people experience Saturn in this negative form. Those people take life's negative experiences under-ground, where they later become self-defeating mechanisms.

At some point, regulation by others is no longer germane. Adolescence is a time when young people make efforts to establish their autonomy, and as adulthood approaches Saturn begins to work from a more unconscious base. If the rules and patterns of worldly life have taught the individual a proper 'place', to have self-respect, and appreciate peace and order, then Saturn comes to represent and support mature love, common sense, con-science and knowledge based on wisdom. If life's experiences reinforce the negative face of Saturn it is difficult to achieve maturity. A need for status, self-justification and superiority replace balanced behaviour, and the psyche senses a distinct lack of love and harmony, a chill that reaches the depths of soul.

Thus Saturn reflects the formative years, imprinting on the psyche as on a wax template the model that will regulate and determine future attitudes and social behaviour. The wheel of life turns, either with monotonous sameness or with steady and worthwhile growth. Saturn represents the progressive and marked phases of psychic development. An individual can be something of a psychic scapegoat, carrying guilt and fears not his own but projected by the group, and may need to face such patterning in dreams as well as in conscious life.

Saturn regulates and inhibits but at the same time enables compromise and security in growth. Once a person is able to set aside scapegoat response mechanisms, responsibility becomes a matter of choice – dreams often reveal the negative template, and can empower the dreamer to reach for the more positive experience of Saturn.

Erin Sullivan says of the Saturn transit – a period in time when Saturn is passing over sensitive points in the horoscope – 'It can leave one with a profound sense of harmony and balance, a feeling of proportion and right order; of peace, goodwill and generosity; or it can unleash a sensation of dread, of having been pursued by forces beyond the boundary for some nameless crime; of feelings of guilt, of having left something undone or, worse, having done something unspeakable.'[4] Letting go of dread and fear of the unspeakable, of resentment and blame, allows us to access harmony.

Atonement, if we view it in the guise of heavy responsibility, is the collective guilt and fear that we carry in Saturn. This can be reinforced by threatening, moralizing and dictatorial dogmas experienced through unproductive and institutionalized religion, and through political regimes that set themselves in authority over life. In this way, Saturn can be the antithesis of Jupiter, and it is this barrier that Jupiter seeks to transcend. The word atonement can also be read as at-one-ment, meaning individuation; religion comes from a root meaning realignment. While the inner Saturn reflects all our personal terrors, it also reflects deep, abiding and committed love, contained and maintained in inner peace within the soul 'home', and can be reassuring and imply that atonement has been achieved.

In the dream chart, Saturn as the dominant planet points out the inhibitions and fears that cripple conscious enjoyment of life. It regulates the dreamer's activities from an inner perspective. It may also tell whether the dreamer is being ruled by feelings and attitudes which emanate from self-regulatory abilities or belong to a pattern of inheritance, good or bad. Dreamers may need to confront the devils – guilt, fear and cruelty – that plague them as part of the healing process of dreaming. They are often aware of being vulnerable and unsure in a dream. Saturn's connection with time and tradition is as a storehouse of experience, and the dreamer can bring to the surface many old and often collective images. There is no doubt that the conscious experiences that wound and scar the psyche carry forward throughout life. The 'bad dream', where death often features, is common in Saturn dreams and connects both to current experiences and to old burdens. Habitual attitudes, strongly reinforced by family and society, are hard to break, and there is always a risk of denial of the opportunity for at-one-ment.

Saturn embodies the tendency to hold on to old guilt and limiting patterns, because they are predictable; even the negative can seem 'safe'. The task of the waking dreamer is to use the wisdom revealed in the dream and *work* consciously with it to make changes. If dreamers cannot confront the negative images in the dream, they will continue to experience rigidity in waking life, as their 'fate' will seem set in concrete. If one can understand the self-defeating mechanisms shown in the dream, one can take steps to revise and refine and overcome barriers.

Saturn also represents ancient wild nature and resonates to the wisdom of the ages, to personal maturity and authority over life, to survival, understanding and acceptance of death, pain and rebirth as a natural cycle in nature. It opens up potential for real healing of the instinctive self, to balance that which in conscious life might be the cause of pain. It is with Saturn in the dream world that we can access a sense of deep, abiding harmony and self-worth, of accord and absolution.

5

Transpersonal Planets –
beyond the Threshold

O age of man! Aquarius,
Transmuter of all things base,
'Son of Man in the Heavens,
with sun illuminated face'.
Our journey was long and weary,
with pain and sorrow and tears,
But now at rest in thy Kingdom,
we welcome the coming years.
George Washington Carey

THE 'TRANSPERSONAL' PLANETS

Astrologers group the three most distant plants, Uranus, Neptune and Pluto, under the terms 'generational', 'collective' or 'transpersonal' planets. Partly, this is because their distances from the central Sun astronomically are so great that their positions in astrological signs are lengthy and so are common in generational charts for a number of years. Uranus is in one sign for seven years, Neptune for fourteen and Pluto, depending on its place along the ecliptic, is in a sign for anywhere from thirty-two years (Taurus) to twelve (Scorpio). Symbolically, their significance is also 'distant' from the conscious core of identity, the Sun or ego – rooted in ancient collective-unconscious motifs and meaning – the unconscious depths of the individual psyche. They cannot be seen by the naked eye, and thus symbolically are invisible to the 'I'. To understand these planets is to reach back far beyond the scope of personal, material and historical experience, and get in touch with their ancient and collective meaning.

These are the archetypes that are constants within human experience and are rooted in human origins, yet reach upward to spiritual heights. As each of these planets was discovered, their intrinsic significance has emerged, rediscovered in a sense through collective consciousness. Their significance for potentials in human nature has become better understood and they will continue to affect the human psyche as future potentials, not realities, because they have no known boundaries.

Saturn represents the boundaries of human awareness, and beyond it lie all the transpersonal planets embedded in what we might also call the superconscious or spiritual dimension. The boundary of Saturn and the regulatory means by which we live our conscious lives separate these planets from personal experience, so they represent deeply unconscious fields of experience, beyond the ego. In this way they correlate with mass shifts in the evolution of collective developments and individuals experience them personally through awareness shifts in unconscious life, projected into worldly activities.

When we try to describe the ancient, deeply embedded archetypes, it is tempting to capture their meaning in personal imagery, but they are best expressed through abstract concepts rather than 'realities'. Personalizing will only take into account, at best, vague and conscious projections, that is, their historical manifestations on to which we hook significance. Outer planetary powers lie so deeply in the collective unconscious that they must be interpreted in their pure form. To reach the depth of meaning in these archetypes we need to view them as gestalt fields of experience, as energy or resonance, not as actuality, regardless of how they might manifest in the worldly life of the individual.

In human history, the unique person, or social movement, has occasionally emerged as a representative of the gestalt of these planets. Such people seem to act as channels for the collective intent of the planets' meaning and focus that meaning into world consciousness. The intellectual genius of Einstein and the development of technology personify the planet Uranus; Michelangelo, Van Gogh, Martin Luther King, can be seen to represent the planet Neptune; Hitler, Gandhi and Freud correlate with the power of Pluto; yet each of these individuals expressed the planets' powers through a shift in consciousness of the masses.

These planetary symbols maintain their ancient characteristics, 'safe' behind the boundary of our complete understanding, the core significance only overlaid loosely by individual experience. They are those facets of the personality not conditioned by personal and social expectation. They connect to our origins, the cradle of civilization and our basic reason for being. Their meaning is ancient and collective.

We must remember the common, collective root when interpreting the dream chart. We access those collective roots in the unconscious – most effectively in dreams. The dream message cuts through the thin veneer of personal experience and reaches deep into the symbolic dimensions common to all dreamers to reveal hitherto unknown facets of the personality and life potential. Through them we may access our own potential for genius, artistry or destruction – for liberation, transcendence or transformation.

Because these planets travel in orbits around the Sun at such enormous distances they transit the natal horoscope slowly, passing over sensitive points of personal planets in the horoscope for long periods of time. Astrologers define the orbits of Uranus, Neptune and Pluto as 'outer planet transits'; on passing over sensitive points in the horoscope, they seem to correspond with mirrored events and conscious experiences. Sweeping changes in consciousness and waking-life experiences correspond to these transit movements, but unconscious shifts are occurring too. At the same time, the faster, more central planets are also travelling, comparatively at lightning speed. Compare the passage of the planet Pluto with that of the Moon as it transits the natal horoscope and you can get some idea of the difference. Pluto circles the horoscope (the entire 360° zodiac) in approximately 250 years – the Moon monthly.

When an individual experiences outer, transpersonal planets' transits to natal planets, they are also experiencing the more brief contacts of inner personal planets to natal planets. These faster-moving transits show in the dream chart but are rarely taken into account in the study of transits' cycles. For example, at the same time that a dreamer has, in a dream chart, the Moon or Mercury in aspect to Uranus, they are also experiencing other transits to the natal chart. Imagine that transiting Uranus is making an aspect to, say, the natal Sun.

The person, in their worldly life, faces some dilemma that synchronizes with this planetary transit. There is a link, a connection with the symbolic meaning encapsulated in the planet that is common to both the dream chart and the natal chart, that will in some way be significant for the dreamer in terms of his current waking experiences. The dream chart will illustrate some unconscious manifestation or shift in line with the context of the outer planets' transits experience. It might inspire the dreamer with knowledge from 'outside of the self' that is of great significance in waking life, and empower him to greater understanding of his current dilemma. At this point we need to continue our examination of the planets' meanings in the dream chart, and we will deal in a later chapter with the implications of the natal chart, when we examine the synastry between the dream and the natal chart.

Uranus

This planet resonates to the principles of chaos, revolution, liberation, progress and change. The words alone indicate a dynamic, not a static quality, implying that we are on the move, changing and evolving to reach a higher perfection, both collectively and individually. Uranus represents abstract concepts, mutation, unpredictable and explosive thoughts and actions waiting to be aroused and brought into consciousness, to rise and meld with consciousness to give an 'idea' of a more progressive and exciting life, and a sense of a more enlightened self. It is the spirit of liberation from the bounds of conscious strictures, the freedom to 'be' what one might be, even if that means flying off at a tangent from the accepted norms of worldly life and structure of the personality.

Uranus works through the principle of mental power, by stimulating the spirit of intuitive thought, which is not rational in the commonly accepted sense. It is the point of departure for a sense of new and previously unknown experiences, which might enable the individual and the group to create and improve on what has become outmoded. It challenges the status quo, and taps into an unconsciousness that is still in potential.

We can observe Uranus being acted out in the young, who frequently rebel against the restrictions imposed by parents, teachers, and society at a time when Uranus is transiting potent points in their charts. The 'teenager' as a phenomenon emerged when society became more aware of the need to express the 'inner anarchist' in the late 1950s, a time when the western world was complacent, and social structures were superficial and aligned with unworkable philosophies. The concept of father/breadwinner, mother/ housekeeper simply did not work after the war years, yet society clung to outmoded patterns of family behaviour and young people tapped in to the gestalt of Uranus, bursting into society as a hitherto unknown subculture. This is not to say that society had not previously experienced Uranus – indeed it had – but the teenager phenomenon serves to illustrate the power of Uranus to make sweeping changes in the psyche of the collective.

The 'mid-life crisis' frequently occurs when Uranus is opposing its natal place in the astrology of individuals between the ages of thirty-seven and forty-two. It allows the individual to express repressed or unconfirmed urges from years earlier, and can awaken the individual to his unfulfilled potential. When worldly progress is not apparent, progress does not occur in the spirit life of an individual. Static life conditions arrest spiritual growth, until the time that Uranus energies can emerge from the unconscious and a crisis occurs. Out of that crisis emerge change and progress. Crisis can be a painful experience for those who do not anticipate change, or fail to recognize the revolutionary spirit within. It is the point where we have the opportunity for an enlightenment beyond commonplace concerns. Since its discovery this planet has come to symbolize the spirit of humanitarian concerns, coinciding with world revolutions proclaiming 'freedom for the common man'. It connects to the spirited rebellion against oppressive conditions, and the same urge can also operate as a desire to be freed of some facet of the common self.

Uranus' symbolism is diametrically opposite to that of Saturn and so there is a constant struggle between the urge to go beyond structured living, with its rules and constraints, and the urge to settle down, live by the rules and accept the status quo. Saturn represents all that is 'normal', conventional and proven by time and tradition, while Uranus represents the 'abnormal', unconventional, radical and eccentric experience, unproven and focused on futuristic directions. Regulations are firmly in place and imprinted in behavioural patterns, giving comfort in their sameness, yet the Uranus side of the psyche constantly knocks at the door of accepted norms, challenging and exciting the very structure of conformity.

Reality, as we know it, is 'surrounded' by chaos – even at our most complacent moments we need to be able to anticipate change, to sense intuitively the critical instability of life. Different individuals may view this with creative excitement or with a paralysing fear of the unknown. Since the discovery of Uranus, there has been an acceleration in technological developments, in improved living conditions in advanced countries. Medicine, science and art have all developed at high speed. We surf the Internet like explorers of old. As Uranus continues to influence the collective psyche, we see clearly that we can no longer assume that life depends on cause and effect. Possibly the only predictable fact is that life is unpredictable!

Uranus is capable of promoting behaviour that is so far beyond the pale that it is completely deviant, eccentric and destructive. Because it works through mental channels, it represents that side of us that pays no heed to matters of the heart. This results in our capacity to be heartless, vindictive and inhuman. Its connection with the intellect gives it an affinity with

Mercury – a rather high-tensile nerve conduit. In astrology we consider Uranus a 'higher octave' of Mercury and as such it takes mental activity one step beyond the factual to the inventive, from rational to irrational and from reason to paradox. It takes the mind into the realms of both genius and aberration – many noted geniuses had their ideas condemned as deviant, only later to have those same ideas accepted.

When Uranus is the potent planet in the dream chart it is as though the dreamer is being called beyond his limits to a place where all things are possible. It is a call from the etheric, where chaos exceeds the bounds of time and space, and so these dreams may have elements of clairvoyance, beyond the limits of linear time. Dreams can also act to release the suppressed, pent-up desire to break the chains of self-defeating worldly conditions. We often have little understanding of just how limiting certain facets in mundane life are until a Uranian dream astonishes us. Such dreams shake the dreamers out of their complacency and force them to look at the life situations that are denying them their full potential. The dream may confront dreamers with their social, racial, sexual and moralistic perspectives, and force a review of their biases and prejudices. It may remind them of youthful visions and dreams, before daily responsibilities, prejudicial attitudes and limiting guilt reflexes cut off their creativity. It may indicate what they need to integrate into consciousness, not as a *fait accompli* but as seeds of creative change. It may reveal that, in order to progress, one must challenge the reliable, outgrow and break with the predictable, take a risk and seek for uniqueness and individuality.

There is often a sense of revelation, a metaphorical cry of 'Eureka' as the dreamer awakes. Answers are found to questions that have puzzled the dreamer, innovative solutions to difficult situations. Dreamers discover aspects of the self and of life unknown until the dream. We see this in Anna's dream, which she named 'resurrection' – 'I dreamed I was an anthropologist on a field trip to Africa. We came across a village where there were piles of corpses. I heard a weak cry and pulled at a body of a woman. A small boy was alive and said, "You angel, now I have a chance to live." He was the only person alive.'

At the time of the dream Anna was a second-year university student. She contacted me on the same day as the dream, saying that she had decided to change her focus to study subjects which would be more challenging and exciting. She said she intuitively 'felt right' in making the changes. She wondered about the dream and felt it was instrumental in making her

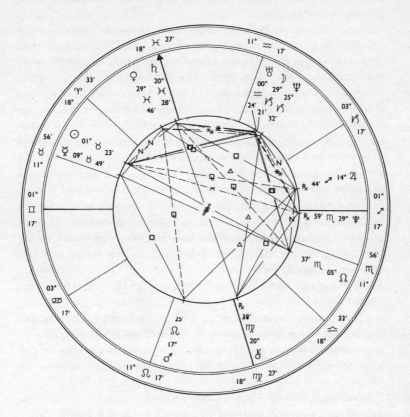

6. Anna's Resurrection Dream (illustrating Uranus potency)

decision, as if it had inspired her actions in some way, because she could not get it out of her mind.

The chart shows the Moon in conjunction to Uranus and Neptune in the eighth house, septile Saturn on the mid-heaven, sextile Pluto. The Moon is about to change from earth, practical and perhaps static, to air, abstract and intellectual, and is at the last degree of the sign, showing endings, a 'death' and rebirth. The Moon's position highlights Anna's need for functional change. Whenever the Moon is about to change elements, there is a rather critical point which links very diverse functions; while it is not common to find the Moon at this critical point in the dream chart, when it is, it serves to focus on the functional shift illustrated by the elements and adds to the need for change. In this case, the shift from earth to air is from introverted and stable to extroverted and exploring. (Mass transformed into energy!) The final quarter phase with the Sun indicates something is ready for integration into consciousness. Mercury is conjunct the Sun and south node, in the eleventh house, the house traditionally associated with Uranus, square Mars in the third house of learning, education, mind, communication, verbal capacities and environment.

The message is about identity and elimination, and is most potent in the aspect to Mars – the action and decision part of Anna – her dissatisfaction and desire for meaning and excitement being represented by Neptune and Uranus. The dream chart resounds to the need for change, for decisive action and letting go of something which is impeding her progress and of which she is subconsciously aware. No wonder she felt right in making the switch!

Interestingly, the day following Anna's dream, it became known that tribal war had broken out in Rwanda and many people had been found massacred; Anna's dream occurred in Australia at about the same time that the massacres would have been taking place or were being discovered, and there had been no prior media coverage of any unrest.

Neptune

Trying to describe Neptune we use words – 'nebulous', 'vague', 'sensitive', 'atmospheric' – that, in themselves, lack essence or core. Neptune represents mystical and visionary scope and is a gestalt of energy, a feeling rather than an entity. It is associated with the boundless element of water, the sea world and the unconscious realm of imagination. It is fluid, immaterial and mobile, constantly flexing and diverting, running underground, rising in storm, placid and threateningly immobile in dead calm. We are unable to hold an image for long enough to discover a core, for Neptune embodies the power to shift shapes. Images disappear as fast as they reappear in other forms. I am reminded of some of the images created by holograms, of 'virtual reality', of the creative work of computer image makers, where, before our very eyes, a substantial image dissolves and becomes something totally different.

Neptune's principle at a collective level is universal love, and so it implies a yearning for perfection in the human state. Esoterically, it is the higher octave of Venus. In contrast to Venus, Neptune does not require exchange, but simply giving, and so can manifest as self-sacrifice. The essence of its symbolism is dissolution of ego – no easy task for most of us! It is perfect soul experience when expressing unconditional love, utterly unselfish, even sacrificial. We can describe its gestalt as a place or space typified by terms such as heaven, nirvana, otherworld, spiritual dimensions or sacred space.

We encourage our children to reach the Neptunian experience through telling stories of never-never land, fairyland, magic castles, middle earth – landscapes that exist in poetic soul dimensions. We experience feelings we describe as ecstasy, joy, bliss, supreme happiness, enabling the individual to have faith in perfection beyond the body and to believe in the happy ending, the perfect union of prince and princess, the demise of evil.

Nevertheless, Neptune is decidedly deceptive, obsessive and addictive, treacherous if the individual makes its unconscious energy a part of his personal conscious motivation without being aware that nothing lasts, nothing is at it seems and we cannot rely on the planet.

Neptune correlates with altered states of mind or being, and as such represents the magic of transcendence, illusion, but also of delusion – it symbolizes hypnotic states, visionary and mystical experience, hallucinations, religious fervour, drug-induced escape from reality. Neptune represents the dream state to which we all return each night, the first line we cross, without resistance, to enter another dimension. There is another fine line between sanity and madness, and Neptune also represents crossing that line – insubstantial, flexible and permeable, where reality and unreality overlap. We are all familiar with stories of people who believe themselves to be Jesus Christ, Joan of Arc or other notable figures. Society confines these people in places where they live out their fantasies. The dilemma with Neptune is to be able to go beyond the mundane and experience the beauty it offers without sacrificing the capacity to function in the real world.

At its most beautiful, it connects to music, art, poetic language, image, colour, vibration and harmony; it touches on feelings, not rationality, and reaches the depths of soul where it may inspire vision and awaken the senses. It may be the waking 'dream' that becomes the reality of the religious, of the healer, or of the artist, many of whom sacrifice personal life for their 'dream'. It represents the power of prayer, of true charity and humility, of empathy and sympathy with the downtrodden and with feelings of unity with others. The Neptune experience transcends race, religion, colour and creed, education and sex, to unite in a universal bond of brotherly and sisterly love with the collective of which we are a part. Tuning into Neptune is an act of introversion, ecstasy and worldly renunciation. It is 'outside' of the self, beyond the boundaries of worldly awareness, does not seek to change personality structures but to transcend them, to pass through barriers as though they do not exist. To 'connect' fully with the essence of Neptune demands complete submission, a lack of ego, a sense of being out of the confines of the corporeal body, with no awareness of solidity or reality. Then it can be a powerful psychic influence in matters connected to spirituality, imagination, abstract imagery and the search for the perfect state; above all it is accessible in the dream state.

Sleep is a Neptunian state when we let go of any awareness of body, earthly concern and ego consideration. Liz Greene says, 'Neptune opens the floodgates to the experience of the suffering of the world and the agony of the spirit incarnated in flesh. The longing is for release from the body's prison and union with the divine source, whether this is taken in the spiritual sense as God or in a reductive sense as the original unity of the mother's womb.'[1]

Neptune draws the dreamer into unknown and undefined territory, where it speaks in images that have little shape, where the dreamer returns to the collective landscape of soul for renewal, inspiration, healing and the experience of perfect love. The dreamer may experience feelings of ecstasy, awaken to new emotion and retain feelings that can be uplifting. If such feelings are absorbed and integrated into life there is inspiration, renewed faith and hope – a great sea journey of renewal has occurred.

Dreamers may also experience delusionary tendencies, as the dream highlights all the self-deceptive mechanisms embodied in our conscious lives. It may reveal personal 'madness' and point to the untruths we tell ourselves and others, the deception and confusion that we live with day by day. The dreamer may then awake feeling moody, discontented and resentful.

When Neptune is the potent planet in the dream chart, its message is cryptic, often indecipherable except through feelings. Neptune dreams may refer to the deceptive nature of the dreamer but may also be instrumental in bringing inspired knowledge from the soul. Synthesis with other planets will be important, especially so if Neptune is connected to the personal planets, when it will imply some flaw or perfecting process in the personality. It may simply be a dream of spiritual refreshment. Connected to the social planets, it might imply worldly matters, moral and ethical affairs needing close examination. It may warn of deception in day-to-day matters.

Pluto

Pluto also represents a part of the deep unconscious, often the most distant shadowy self. To express the full meaning of Pluto is to tap into a dark void. To describe a void is to negate its meaning, for as soon as we impose form on something that in effect is devoid of form we reduce and restrict its extent. Each new entity, each materialization, idea or reality comes from some dark space and time continuum that we cannot grasp. It did not exist before we gave it form, and so it is with Pluto energy. As with the other collective symbols, we cannot personalize Pluto easily except through an enormous variety of projections. Pluto power presents a gestalt of darkness, a cavern, cauldron, womb or grave from which life springs renewed. It correlates with life, death and resurrection.

Astronomically, the planet is so distant from the Sun that it does not receive any light. From Pluto the Sun would seem to be nothing more than a pale twinkling star among myriad others like it. Symbolically, that means that, from a Pluto-perspective, the Sun is of little importance and its correlation with ego has little significance beyond a faint existence. The Earth and thus symbolically our own hold on worldly values, would appear nothing more than a dust particle. We might play around the edges of Pluto's meaning but we can never fully describe the fathomless depths of the unconscious. Pluto forces us to face how unimportant individual ego matters might be, and how quickly life can be extinguished. We are required to face death and destruction and hope for renewal. With each moment in our lives something dies to make way for something new.

There is pain in birth, death and transmutation. Conscious Pluto experiences draw us into the darkness of loss, grief and anguish, and change us for ever, but this is only a fraction of the mighty force of Pluto. We are reborn into consciousness as different people. The gestalt of Pluto is of destruction and reconstruction. Embedded in its symbolism are the inseminating seeds of new creation awaiting birth. We can view it metaphorically as the fertile primeval swamp to which all life returns, the swamp which gives new life to the dead, and we have an inescapable link with it – even those who live lives seemingly free of trauma will inevitably experience the ultimate Pluto experience.

History has recorded individuals who have been channels for, or representatives of, Pluto power. These individuals have in some way been able to tap into the gestalt to bring forth either reformation or destruction, essentially using the deep subconscious power of the species to cause mass shifts in world experience. Hitler, as mentioned at the start of this chapter, is one example of such an individual. One through whom positive Pluto power emerged was Mohandas Gandhi – a man who was able to immerse personal ego in the pure reformative waters of Pluto and re-emerge as a symbol of his race. In his life, because he had given up personal vanity and ego associations, he became the means by which a nation was reborn. Essentially, these two people tapped into the same gestalt of renewal, but the difference was in the capacity of one to set aside all personal ego considerations and so become the channel for reconciliation, while the other attached the power of Pluto to ego and became an instrument of destruction. Such examples serve to illustrate the power of Pluto, a power capable of changing the face of nations – what then can it do for the individual? Negatively, it carries in its image the potential for violence, genocide, eruptions of devastating emotion, the complete ruination of life as we know it. Positively, it offers opportunity and power to eliminate toxins, break free of bondage and be resurrected in a new life.

When Pluto is the potent planet in dreams it does not invoke images that are nebulous or vague, it invokes those that are active, brooding, deeply significant and emotively charged. Pluto dreams take the dreamer into a place of nightmare or a place in which a new spirit is born. It is not a place of pleasure, but it does promise more fruitful life, once we heed its message. Pluto brings deeply buried complexes, repressed pain, rage, emotions and traumas to the surface, to be reconciled and healed. In dreaming, this can be a powerful 'safe' way to deal with such motifs, needing only that the dreamer accept that healing has occurred. Facing loss and grief and terrible rage is to look deep into the meaning of Pluto; symbolically to look the power in the eye and recognize that renewal is available despite the anguish.

Such dreams will connect us to the deepest primeval *angst*, the separation of nature from the divine, and remind us of the loss of our own immortality.

If such dreams are an uprooting of buried complexes that are ready for transformation, then the dreamer can safely acknowledge destruction of such complexes in the dream state and wake to a sense of catharsis. Along with experiences that have been traumatic, childhood taboos, feelings, desires and instincts that have for one reason or another been denied are also pushed down into the Plutonic realm, and can reappear in dreams. In life, the individual chooses that which he can deal with and deny that which is too painful. In dreams such traumas arise again and can be dealt with in safety. Liz Greene writes, '. . . they are too violent, too vengeful, too bloodthirsty, too primitive and too hot for the average individual to feel much comfort or safety in their intrusion . . . Thus a large slice of childhood falls beneath the censor's knife – those slices which reveal the savage face of the young animal struggling for self-gratification and survival.'[2] So what is suppressed may be the result of experience or of those aspects of the primitive life-and-death struggle embedded in the gestalt of Pluto that we cannot acknowledge or integrate.

Pluto might encourage the dreamer to push away relationships no longer valid, be they personal, sexual or emotional, or relationships with material objects and situations to which he has emotional attachment. It indicates that the primitive survival instinct is alive and vital, and accessible to the dreamer, and shows that for further survival, at some level of psychic or worldly activities, the dreamer needs to tap into the possibly 'violent and vengeful'[3] urges within. It represents individuation in the constant rebirth of facets of the self, drawing on the two most distant symbols, Sun and Pluto. Through Pluto dreams we make connection with our darker selves and ultimately face our own shadows.

What we see in Plutonian dreams is not savoury – we may be tempted to deny that we are what we see, but the images emanate with a purpose: they give us the opportunity to set aside our concepts of status or importance and face our potential for evil; they allow us to destroy preconceived ideas about our lives and replace them with new ones. Greene continues, 'Confronted with Pluto, we meet our abhorrent, our insatiable passions: the impossible repetitive patterns of struggling with something only to meet it again and again.'[4] The message of Pluto in a dream is that it is time for fundamental and absolute change – something old, long held, perhaps 'abhorrent' has been, will be or must be destroyed to make way for the new.

The Moon's Nodes

Nodes are the point at which the Moon crosses the extension of the plane of the earth's orbit – otherwise known as the ecliptic. There are two nodes, each the point of contact made in the Moon's movement in the north or south celestial latitudes; astrologers call them the north node and the south node of the Moon. The nodes connect Sun, Moon and Earth in a symbolic relationship of ego, soul and earthbound reality. We can therefore interpret them as representing the conscious and unconscious journey through life, the associations made with life experiences and relationships with others on the earthly plane. Traditionally, astrologers describe the nodes in a variety of ways, associate them with destiny, or 'karma', with past lives, with groups and associations, with the urging of ego to achieve and with the capacity to draw into life experiences anything that is beneficial to the individual soul. The serpentine pattern drawn from the nodal transits, from the point of view of earth, is a graphic illustration of the circumambulation of the individuation process and implies that the process takes place within the psychic and bodily reality of the person.

The north node is also called the Dragon's Head and the south node the Dragon's Tail. The symbolic imagery entrenched in the idea of a dragon is of a fire-breathing monster that fiercely guards a cave in which there is a captured maiden. The maiden can only be released by the bravery of the hero, who on his way must fight the dragon to rescue the maiden. So the dragon can represent an aspect of the self that can be viewed as inflated ego. Only by defeating this negative manifestation can the cave of the unconscious be reached and the symbolic pure soul released. It is an essential, one way or another, to all stories and myths of the hero's journey, representing the achieving of balance between ego and soul. The hero then finds his true vocation – his quest involves the release of pure soul so that it may become an active part of life and the individuation process.

The nodes, then, represent a sense of vocation, mission or calling that is above material or ego intent. Nodes do not have mass, they are not planets but sensitive points with no energy or gestalt representation – they are specific to the individual. Their meaning is in the potential, not the fact. They point to the 'way' or the road through life that the individuated self takes and the ego dragons he fights along the way.

Everyone in life is making some progress and in the dream chart the nodes express the path to perfecting ourselves. The north node is the quintessence of where we might be heading, what we are drawing on to promote meaningful bonding of ego and soul within the reality of worldly life. The south node represents that which is no longer relevant in the process and which the psyche should abandon. The nodes can indeed express destiny, associations and experiences in worldly life, and when the nodes are significant in the dream chart, they give some indication of their value to the psychic process. Their meaning is at an instinctive level, just as the process of individuation is an instinctive urge. In the dream chart, nodes do not express any energy, or 'speak'. Their significance is that of the 'way of the dragon'. The nodes in the dream chart express how close or how far we have strayed from the instinctive way. They act as signposts to individuation. Aspects to other planets will be highly significant, the symbolic 'message' of those planets will have a bearing on the instinctual journey.

The contacts imply wisdom and deeply significant intuitive knowledge. Howard Sasportas, describing the individuation process, says, '. . . somewhere deep within us there is primordial knowledge or preconscious perception of our true nature, our destiny, our abilities and our "calling" in life. Not only do we have a particular path to follow but, on an instinctive level, we know what that is.'[5]

The dreamer may experience a reassuring sense of his own individuation, particularly when aspects are harmonious, and, if aspects are tense, may find himself able to learn something from his dream about where he might be taking a wrong turn in conscious life and so rediscover the true path. He may also discover that the message is specific to practical and worldly matters, associations and decisions, that ultimately affect the whole life journey.

Chiron

We cannot strictly call Chiron an outer planet, for its maverick orbit alternates between Jupiter and Saturn, and then between Saturn and Uranus. In the same way, it alternates between the symbolic boundaries of worldly consciousness and beyond those boundaries to the unconscious. Astrologers have since its discovery connected its meaning with that of the 'wounded healer'. Chiron is not so much a psychic entity as a pattern of woundedness and healing.

As an emerging archetype Chiron is now being clothed in personal imagery, the core of its symbol concurrent with the wounding of and awareness of the fragility of earth and the survival of its people. In a very real sense it connects to the physical and psychological woundedness of individuals bridging the psychic and somatic levels of being. We have much to learn about and from Chiron as it becomes more integrated in the astrological pantheon. Its recent discovery means that the human psyche is still struggling to understand its message. Much admirable work has been done over a few short years, principally by Melanie Reinhart.[6] Perhaps Chiron's entry into the solar system is a temporary state and, once we learn the meaning of it, it may leave our system again.

In the natal chart it represents a potential for being wounded and for healing, the wound first triggered in early childhood and carried throughout life. It connects to the first sense of being 'different' from or abandoned by the family, the crowd, of not 'fitting in' to socially acceptable mores that give comfort and security. The wound is both physical and psychological. As the planet alternates between visible and invisible, it does so symbolically between conscious and unconscious, thus representing the link between psyche and soma, as well as the capacity to wound and the capacity to heal, and such symbols surface, submerge and surface again. The inner Chiron defines a way of dealing with and healing wounds, based on the homoeopathic principle that what harms heals. Dreams when Chiron is potent are a reworking of early feelings and reactions that enable the dreamer to gain self-knowledge and turn that knowledge into wisdom. In similar ways to Jupiter, Chiron acts as a bridge, but while Jupiter bridges personal and social realms, Chiron links the differentiated parts of the animalistic and spiritual self.

Intrinsic to its meaning, Chiron woundedness may be the woundedness we are *meant* to carry, so that we may learn more about ourselves, our reactions and our relationships, and are then able to distinguish the differentiated ego and soul, mind and body, and meld the differentiated parts into a whole. Its woundedness is the primitive and instinctive expression that can be equated to the instinctive knowledge of separation that is the catalyst for the process of individuation. The psychology of Chiron indicates that early wounding occurs at an instinctive and crude, immature level of the psyche, and from it we learn much about respect for our own primitive and infantile selves; we also learn that primitive reactions and responses may become 'civilized' or individuated with time.

Ken Wilbur, in his book *Up from Eden*,[7] postulates several stages of psychic evolution, beginning with the 'Uroboric'[8] stage, of bliss and fusion, when there is no differentiation between mind and body. This is the stage of primeval unwounded instinctual self. In a chronological sense, this equates with the prenatal and early infancy period – a time without understanding of past, present or future. There is great vulnerability to wounding.

The second stage is what he calls 'Typhonic'.[9] At this level, awareness of mind and body, ego and soul awareness, begin to differentiate, but are not fully separate from primeval instincts. It is at this time that manifestation of woundedness occurs at both the physical and psychic levels, and is the trigger that enables us to recognize the distinction between the two parts of self and experience the pain of separation. During this phase, correlating with early childhood, we turn inward, so woundedness becomes embedded.

A third stage might occur with maturity. Wilbur names it the 'Existentialist'[10] or 'Centaur' level. At this stage the individual rises above his differentiated self. He is aware of and takes responsibility for his own woundedness, becomes wiser, more accepting and so begins to deal with his own woundedness, owning it. There is opportunity for great understanding, acceptance and sharing of insights and wisdom at this stage. We access it in dreaming, even though we may not yet have reached this stage in worldly affairs. This is the phase of dealing with both the psychic and physical levels of dis-ease. Facing wounds of separation, fears of abandonment and pain in dreams is a way of tapping into the original wounded self, bridging the differentiated self and unconsciously healing the individuated self.

The dreamer is able to recognize and resolve the wound as part of the process of growth, and on waking he can be conscious of and forgive those conditions that caused woundedness. Hence the dreamer reaches a turning-point in psychic life. Resolution does not deny the negative but integrates and forms a relationship with it. This Wilbur names the 'Atman'[11] stage. At the Atman stage, we are able to forgive and accept that which we cannot change or heal. With Chiron, many become locked into, and never consciously transcend or get into relationship with, their wounded side. When Chiron is activated in dreams it brings awareness of pain and woundedness in our psychic life. Dreams invoke images that represent the wounded inner child but also the mature, wise self. The dreamer may relive the pain, but will experience the healing. The dream's message is from the profoundly wise and instinctive part of the self. It may indicate that physical health is in need of attention.

Chiron dreams also bring knowledge that is deeply intuitive. Chiron answers questions and gives advice and will often emerge in dreams at times when we are confronted, in life, with choices. There is an intuitive capacity for prophecy embedded in the psyche of humankind, lost as life became 'civilized' and time became linear. Dreams often hark back to buried and collective knowledge. Chiron dreams are revealing in their ability to remind dreamers that the wisdom and knowledge sought in waking life is within them, or to point out where dreamers might seek and find that wisdom. Contacts with the social planet, Jupiter, will tend to relate to matters concerning wisdom and learning, while those to Saturn will tend to access the wounded self.

6

Houses – Mandala of Self

*The moonlight does not show up objects in all their pitiless discreteness and separateness
... but blends in a shimmer the near and the far, magically transforming little things
into big things ... softening all colour in a bluish haze and blending the nocturnal
landscape into an unsuspecting unity ...*   Dr C. G. Jung

THE HOUSES

The twelve houses in astrology define zones of life experience and are
multi-levelled in that each house includes developmental, spiritual, mundane,
emotional and intellectual layers. They are derived from the time, date and
location of an individual's birth and represent a continuum of experience
both conscious and unconscious from the perspective of that moment in
time. Thus, they define both waking and dreaming, conscious and unconscious areas of whole life experience. For the purposes of examining the
dream experience, the position of the Moon in these houses is critical. It is
not possible to explore all levels of experience, so this chapter is confined
to exploring the meaning of the house through the Moon's location there.

Houses set the scene for the dream experience. They are central to the
purpose, the stage upon which the planetary thespians act out the drama
that is the dream. Houses do not have walls separating them from the
activities of other houses, no matter how diverse the activities may seem.
They interconnect with other fields of experience, particularly with the house
in polar opposition where an 'axis' of interrelated matters forms. However,
in waking life we do tend to compartmentalize life, separating differing
experiences, so that we forget the idea that each experience will ultimately
touch on and affect other areas of life. In the sleeping state, false walls fall
down and there is a free flow between houses. We associate each house
with an element and a planetary meaning too, so that the expression of the

planets 'affairs' are a part of the house experience. For example, the first house connects to fire and the planet Mars, and the seventh house to air and the planet Venus. Both these planets are 'personal' planets, so meaning develops between those houses at a 'personal' level, with an exchange, or polarity, between self-will and personal ego desires in the Mars-associated first house and the capacity to receive and reflect the desires of another in the Venus-associated seventh house. Hence this first/seventh house axis develops through personal relationships.

The time of the dream determines the house position of the Moon in the dream chart. It is as though the Moon stimulates dreaming when it is in a particular house. Thus, specific areas of the psyche and life experience are brought to the dreamer's attention and come into focus as the intent of the dream. Understanding that house, its emotional sensors, its connections with relationships, psychological urges and motivations, enables us to define the reason for dreaming. Light manifests in two ways, from its source and through a projected beam, so the beam 'lands' at some point distant from the source. In the dream chart, the source is the Moon in a particular house filling that house with passive yet focused light, revealing all that the house means. We might imagine the Moon entreating the dreamer to look at the hidden places and subtle undertones of meaning in the house. The projected beam picks out those themes connected to the house opposite and confirms the interrelationship between the polar opposites. It links associated matters between the opposing houses and, by illuminating them, effectively forces something of their meaning to the surface. The Moon's light serves to bring awareness to the dreamer and contains no message except to show that 'this is what the dream is about'.

The First and Seventh Houses

The first house is the house connecting to persona, the mask worn as a protective and coping mechanism in conscious life. Persona, according to Jolande Jacobi, citing Jung, is 'a functional complex which has come into existence for reasons of adaptation, but by no means is it identical with individuality'.[1] She continues, 'The Function complex of Persona is exclusively concerned with the relation to the object . . . a compromise between individual and society as to what man should appear to be . . .'.[2] It combines, then, personal, social and environmental matters, all that is extraneous to the whole self, a face shown to others. It is an essential component of consciousness allowing the individual to cope with temporal life. In the unconscious there is no need of a mask or barrier between the self and the environment. Jacobi continues, 'A properly fitting and well-functioning persona is essential to psychic health and indispensable if the demands of the environment are to be met successfully.'[3] When the Moon is in the first house it might reveal aspects of persona that are not functioning well and so ensure that adjustment and maintenance is taking place at an unconscious level so that the environmental stresses are met successfully on waking.

This house is associated with the desires and drives to achieve something in life that is entirely personal, to strive and struggle with the world and its demands, to engage in personal goals and make a statement to the world that one exists. Mars is the planet we associate with the first house and implicit in that planet is the idea of externalizing and striving to fulfil the desires of the hero self. Fire is the element that underpins the house and it expresses the cardinal or initiating quality. The world and its importance to the individual, the ways in which we enter into the mainstream of conscious living, are all first-house associations. The instinct for personal survival is strong in the first house; such survival, being independent of others, is the embodiment of 'being' in a unique sense of separateness and non-attachment in worldly life. The person might identify the world with a sense of it being his own personal sphere and so it is that the first house expresses that which is very close to worldly activity, to the struggles and battles with which the individual deals in his life journey.

There is a subtle link with the polar-opposite seventh house. The unconscious needs and seeks another person in life with whom to cooperate, someone who can reflect and appreciate the efforts made in life and can share in the victories. The Moon in the first house of the dream chart shows where personal coping mechanisms may need examination or be unconsciously adapted to cope better with changing circumstances in the waking environment. The seventh house comes into focus as representative of the partner in worldly life. It brings awareness of unconscious needs and desires for relationship with others, and of how such needs fit with, and give purpose to, personal efforts to survive, achieve and relate to others in the wider environment. 'Others' may be an individual, a partner, an audience or indeed any other humans with whom we make close personal contact through relationship. Relationship is an exchange of energy, a meeting and joining of two individuals who touch and affect each other mutually. The dreamer's end of the relationship is the first house.

As there is no disconnection between houses, the experience of the first house can express entirely individual goals, but will always link with its opposite house, the seventh. There would be no need for personal goals if there were no other people in a person's life. The first house describes the person's contribution to any relationship, harmonious or otherwise, whether he is aware of his part in it or not.

Because of the Moon's symbolic connection with nurturing and the principle of emotional growth, change and the cycles in life, in a passive way it will bring added benefit to the dreamer, by encouraging him or her to grow and change his perspective of relationships. If one's relationships are stressed, then the Moon in the first house encourages one, by highlighting one's attitudes and contributions, to look at one's part in the relationship. Emotional sensors are close to the surface in a first-house dream and it is not easy to be objective when working with the dream, as the dreamer re-establishes defence mechanisms upon waking.

The dream might ideally result in conscious action, recognition and acceptance of the need for a change of attitude, but is equally likely to result in the 'blame' for waking dilemmas being projected on to the partner. There can be an energetic denial of personal involvement in the dream message as the dreamer refuses to face the contents of the hidden aspects of their psyche, those unclaimed motifs of the personality which are brought into focus by the seventh house. Compromise is not easy in the first house but the resolution of partnership issues, their consequent adjustments in waking life and the greater interchange in intimate matters are the potential rewards of such a dream.

When the Moon is in the seventh house it will indicate that the dreamer needs to see the partner more clearly. It illustrates the partner's contribution to the relationship, what one might experience in a fair and balanced exchange, emanating from the other person. It will bring images of another, showing qualities one might never have imagined or seen in waking life. The seventh house indicates any circumstance or relationship requiring exchange, compromise, equal balance, rational judgement and accord, and so involves business relationships as well as marriage partners. It connects to waking matters where there may be a dispute or possibility for contractual agreement, and points to ways towards agreement and amicable settlement. The Moon in the seventh house will direct the dreamer to examine the dynamics of the relationship and the other person involved. It shows that change is occurring in a partner and hence in the partnership through that person's contribution.

As mentioned, the seventh house is also the house that connects to the self in its more hidden themes. The dream may bring to light facets of the personality that the dreamer either cannot face or does not rightfully claim. These are just as likely to be affirmative and favourable aspects of the personality as 'shadow' motifs, and quite often when the Moon is here, the dreamer becomes aware of capabilities and faculties hitherto dormant in waking life. If the dreamer, in daily life, projects his unfulfilled or unclaimed potential on to the partner, then in dreams he might recognize and reclaim what is rightly his. The Moon's light is gentle but insistent and will seek out all the corners of the seventh house, revealing, as with all houses, both its positive and negative potential.

Working with dreams involving the first-house/seventh-house axis needs objectivity, the capacity to confront characteristics either of the self or of one's partner that could be difficult to deal with. A dreamer may see attributes in the partner or relationship that are uncomfortable or which he may have denied or avoided in waking life. For example, if one conceives that a partner is less than truthful, or is not making a fair contribution to the partnership, or in some way is contributing to a lack of harmony, one may nevertheless pretend that all is well in the relationship in order to avoid confrontation.

The seventh house is associated with Venus, the element air and the cardinal quality of initiation and so represents the dreamer's capacity for objective cooperation or compromise, for exchange with a partner. Thus it represents what he might fairly expect to receive from the partner – the more one avoids facing the truth in waking life, or avoids dealing with problems, the more likely it is that, in dreaming, images will arise that force one to see the truth. An example of this is Gloria's cream-cake dream.

The Moon in the seventh house brings awareness of either Gloria's partner's part in the relationship or indicates some unowned shadow energy which Gloria herself might need to reclaim. It is in a square aspect to Saturn in the ninth house, so that planet is involved in the reason for dreaming – associated with limits and barriers, self-defeating qualities, family expectations and concerns experienced through the partner. Briefly, there is something in waking life that Gloria identifies as a restricting force and she unconsciously 'assigns' responsibility for this limiting condition to her partner. The Moon is in a trine aspect to the Sun and Venus, both in the second house, so the

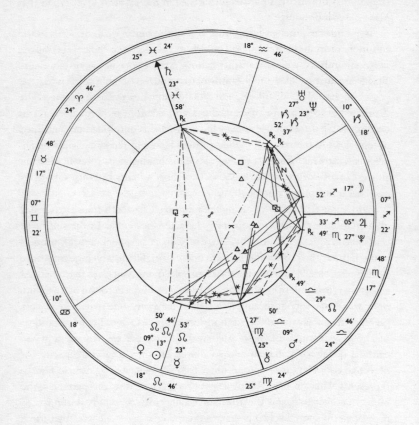

7. Gloria's Cream-cake Dream (illustrating seventh-house potency)

dream also draws attention to Gloria's sense of her own identity and her personal value standards.

The Moon is in fire and is in a house associated with air, so both an intuitive and rational resolution might be found in the dream and Gloria could be imbued with resolve, so that on waking she may feel the urge to deal with any problem in her marriage or business associations. Mercury in the third house is square to Pluto in the sixth house. This is a forceful message — Pluto is compelling feelings and thoughts to the surface, deep seated, long lasting ones, so suppressed that Gloria only now articulates and recognizes them through the dream. Some aspect of the Pluto self emerges from the darker regions to be faced in this dream. The message calls for a powerful and forceful change to be wrought in a circumstance of waking life that is over-structured and unrewarding, creating barriers, guilt and resentment, and is reflected in Gloria's marriage partnership.

The Moon's position encourages Gloria to examine her partner, her partnership agreements and exchanges, and her partner's contributions to problems in the relationship, and may lead her to uncover some facet of her partner that is not entirely comfortable. She may also see some aspect of her own self that she would prefer to keep hidden. The 'safe' way to deal with problems is in dreaming.

Saturn's connection is by its ninth-house position — the Moon draws attention to her feelings of being blocked from attaining a higher level of self and a higher level of educational and developmental growth because of something in the partnership. It identifies that something in the partner's contribution to the marriage may be barring Gloria from achievement and she resents it, but does not articulate it in waking life. The ninth house connects to Gloria's higher mind and desire to expand and, in the dream, is also linked to the partner's communicative capacities, to his relationships with his siblings, his morality and ethics, the structural basis of his education and mental patterns, his environment in childhood, and the consequences of these themes on Gloria.

The seventh house unconsciously motivates the following eighth house, which is where personal and partnership battles emerge, and this dream, because of the danger embedded in the square of Mercury and Pluto, implies that a battle is about to erupt. Mercury is 'speaking' for Pluto and, in collusion with the Moon, is saying that it is time to bring suppressed matters to the surface and either transform or end them. Gloria dreams: 'I was preparing food for a crowd of people who appeared to have come from a funeral. A fat man with cream cake around his mouth came into the kitchen and demanded more food as everything had been eaten. I checked the plates as I didn't believe it possible and found many more fat people gobbling cream cake, all with it smeared around their faces. The fat man was very belligerent, demanding more, more. My friend appeared and told me that no matter how much I provided, those people would never be satisfied. I woke to hear the dog barking and the clock chiming 3 a.m.'

For the astrologer, it is a great privilege to participate in a dreamer's inner work and one must never impose interpretation, but guide the dreamer through the chart and its symbolism to discover why they dreamed the dream and to explore its meaning. In dialogue with Gloria, it emerged that she was exasperated with her husband's siblings, who lived some distance away and were unwilling to care for their sick mother, leaving Gloria to cope on her own. This had been a recurring problem throughout her married life and she felt that her husband's siblings had for too long presumed on her goodwill. She felt that the time spent looking after her mother-in-law meant that she was unable to make progress with her own interests and growth. She also felt that her husband did little to relieve her of the burden. For many years she had resented her in-laws using her, and the way in which they freely interfered in her marriage and their scathing attitude towards her intellectual pursuits.

She felt strongly that she was taking on responsibilities that were not hers but her husband's. Caring for her mother-in-law, unpaid and unappreciated, in the absence of her in-laws, irritated her, but she admitted having done so for years without complaint, an aspect of her personality that she is discovering is self-defeating. This is the same Gloria whose Arab dream we examined on p. 64. The cream-cake dream occurred six months later, towards the end of a phase that had been fraught with problems and changes in Gloria's life.

Gloria was making progress in her job, and was making determined efforts to break through barriers and deal with limiting factors in her conscious life and her psychological make-up. She discussed the dream and its implications with her husband, who, to her surprise, was very supportive and completely understood her dislike of being used by his relatives. He expressed concern that she had not spoken out before and undertook to take full responsibility for any further family concerns that might arise. This was his first indication of the depth of her feelings – he had had no idea how serious the problem was and so he had been content to let things continue as they were for many years. Even though circumstances had changed with Gloria's return to work,

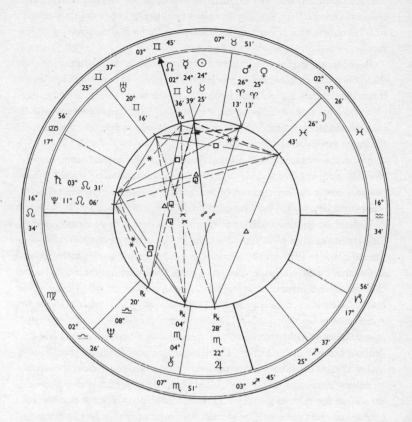

8. Gloria's Natal Chart

she was only now able to recognize the depth of her resentment that her husband had not been the one to activate change, and her own 'martyred' role. He quite willingly undertook to negotiate better arrangements with his family.

The eruption that was imminent and might have been unproductive and destructive was transformed into a cathartic and clearing compromise. Gloria heard Pluto's message and has been able to see how she has a propensity to take on the role of 'responsible person' and so become a victim of her own shadow forces. She now makes conscious efforts to avoid a repeat of the long years of suffering in silence.

At this point examination of Gloria's natal chart (p. 99) and current outer planet transits will give added insight into the dream context, for the context of any dream is the life situation of the dreamer and the outer planet transits express the developmental phase in the dreamer's waking life.

Without going into a full interpretation of Gloria's natal chart, it is not difficult to see that with the Moon in Pisces in the seventh house, and Saturn in the twelfth house, Gloria's natural response is sympathetic and self-effacing, and she is liable to assume responsibility in what she half-jokingly calls her 'Early Christian Martyr mode'. Saturn conjunct Pluto in the twelfth house, square to Chiron, implies conditioned guilt and fears deeply entrenched in her subconscious as well as unconscious desires for personal power. Gloria's formative years were plagued with family sickness and the deaths of several near relatives. The trine aspect between Moon and Saturn makes it easy for Gloria to settle into habitual patterns, redolent of the 'parenting' dynamic and role model – and indeed her mother was responsible for caring for the dying during Gloria's early years. Thus a pattern was established and Gloria an easy subject for such patterning. She operates on automatic once some family crisis of health, decision-making or practical responsibility arises. At the time of the dream, she was experiencing some quite intense outer planet transits, as follows:

Transiting		Natal
♄	☌	☽
♅	□	♀♂
♅	☍	♄
♆	△	☽
♇	☍	☉☿
♇	☌	♃

These transits emerge in her conscious life as tension because of change in family circumstances and have stimulated tension in career areas because she has been feeling 'locked up' by the family situation. Gloria is already tuning in to the potential implicit in these challenges and has had several difficult experiences at this time. Some quite enormous changes have already manifested in her life and Gloria understands that she must view change as a dynamic that begins unconsciously and manifests in 'events' and problems in consciousness.

The planets in the dream chart will make contact with natal planets too. This facet of dream work will be explored in detail later, but Gloria's dream Moon as the significant 'reason' in the dream chart is in opposition to her natal Uranus and in a trine to her natal Pluto — what the Moon is encouraging at the level of natal potential is enormous change. The Moon will, of course, make these aspects every month, but will not necessarily invoke a dream until outer planet transits require it and until Mercury is in a position to bring a potent message. Simply put, it is only when all the component parts are in place at an unconscious level, that Gloria will understand and actively work on the dream's message. As the outer planet transits to her natal chart unfold she is able to take control of her own response mechanisms and make her experiences positive and growing ones.

The Second and Eighth Houses

The second house connects to the quality of the bona fide and recognizable 'proofs' of existence and values in consciousness. Howard Sasportas writes, 'We need more definition, more substance, a greater sense of our own worth and abilities. We need an idea of what it is that we possess which we can call our own. We also should have some notion of what we value, of what we would like to accrue or gain so that we can structure our lives accordingly.'[4] This house, then, is consciously associated with the material manifestations that accrue through our efforts to fulfil those needs, the 'things' we call our own, possessions with which we are able to identify our own sense of worth. It also expresses the unconscious qualities of self-evaluation and well-being, of self-love, as distinguished from the outer expression of beauty, money and objects. It is the house where we measure ourselves by inner and outer resources that become the stock in trade by which we live life.

The Moon in the second house illuminates the dreamer's basic structure of self-worth, self-esteem and values, expressed through the acquisition of material goods as well as in his personal value judgements. The Moon encourages the dreamer to examine the true worth of his resource base. The word 'resource' is not only a measure of material worth but implies inner qualities of resourcefulness, expressed as strengths and abilities on which one can rely. There is a sense of inner assurance and self-reliance, confidence that whatever difficulties life presents, they can be dealt with. The second house is a 'comfort zone', a place of safety, a recognition that one has the resources and capacity to deal with life's challenges.

The body is the entity that gives form and definition to our being – the proof of our existence without which we would not be recognized as being. So this house represents the many physical aspects of our reality. If one does not care for the body as a resource, or respect and give it any value, then the psyche cannot be wholesome. Matters of physical health arise in dreams, as well as connections to sexual expression.

In the second house the self identifies a value structure that is conditioned by the external values by which we live. In the modern world, we are assailed daily by images and expectations expressed through other people's views and attitudes, and such influences affect the individual's attitudes to the body and its functions. Objects and possessions and expressions of love received from intimate and sexual relationships become icons of well-being in conscious life and, in the unconscious, affect the ways we evaluate emotional and psychic security or experience disappointment. Conscious value judgements and daily cultural yardsticks in Western society can be superficial, to say the least. Vanity, the need for the approval of others, affects us daily, seeping into the unconscious and becoming confused with the real paradigms of personal worth. Physical beauty and the sexual mores by which others deem one attractive overlay true worth with the veneer of whatever 'sells' at the time. Thus we receive confusing messages about sexual worth. The second house is associated with Venus, earth and the fixed quality, and so becomes the house where we experience and consolidate unconscious insecurities and fears about our own inner beauty. When the dream Moon is here, it encourages us to not identify with possessions and icons of false value, and shows us a way to perceive true value in ourselves. It shows how we might be unconsciously confused about personal worth through our attachment to perceived sexual measures, material wealth and security.

Dreams can carry themes of deprivation and the struggle to hold on to what is owned or has been earned by one's own efforts. Emotional sensors seek reassurance and attachment in the familiar. The dream, by highlighting habits, can indicate a 'stuck' area of the psyche, an area where one's nature can be resistant to change. Dreams can illustrate how we attach importance to, or depend on, material resources, sexual approval and value judgements of our partner. Quite complex matters can arise in second-house dreams as the polarity with the eighth house pulls in matters of close relationships at a deep-seated and often dramatic level. There can be a combative theme to a dream involving this axis, a life-and-death struggle with another over physical safety and ownership of the person, its objects and resources. Self-worth is measured against the opinions and standards expressed by others in conscious life, but there is a deeper connection — the value judgements expressed in childhood might well be suppressed complexes projected on to the sexual or intimate partner, and can arise in dreams through the association of the planet Pluto with the eighth house.

The eighth-house position of the Moon invites examination of the deeper levels of the unconscious but still connects to the consciousness of the second house. The planet Pluto, the water element and the fixed quality are associated with the eighth house, and when the Moon is here, dreams have an intense emotional content and invoke feelings that can be deeply disturbing. They force us to look at some aspect of our past that has to do with our emotional or sexual responses, an aspect that we might have suppressed or fear to express; these dreams will focus strongly on what we own, or wish to own, in material forms. The Moon will show what painful or difficult experiences one is holding on to for reasons of emotional security, and our desire to control or manipulate others in conscious life to achieve security. It indicates what might have been caught up in our feeling nature, either to drive us or to become trapped and dysfunctional. It also brings images of the beauty and ideas that one may invest in the sexual partner, the unconscious image of one's own second-house potential not yet actuated and projected on to the partner.

Dreams often show opportunities to break away from habitual emotional response patterns and find security in the inner, personal value systems developed through awareness of personal achievement. They imply opportunities to re-evaluate the self. Difficult images arise as the Moon accesses the gestalt of Pluto in this house, so conflicts of a sexual or physical nature arise — life itself might seem to be under threat — and such conflicts can also manifest as conflicts of ownership of resources or inheritance, or as material desires. The nature of relationships along this axis is such that there is pain as well as pleasure, and a dream can seek out those aspects of the self that we experience on a masochistic level, wounds left unhealed that we keep open. The dream might bring to light deep-seated woundedness, pain to which we cling.

Deeply wounded feelings and grief tend to leave one numbed and emotionally paralysed, and often the only way the deeply wounded soul can feel is by reliving some of the more painful episodes of conscious life, for in pain there is often quite an exquisite awareness of feeling that in a paradoxical way assures the person that they are indeed emotionally alive. The dreamer can become locked into a recurring cycle of related dreams, each less painful than the last, so that after some time healing occurs and the dreamer may be able once again to experience joy.

This has occurred for Gloria over a period of time, so her dreams have been used in illustration. Such dreams often happen when outer planet transits to the natal chart are difficult. Loss, both of people in life and of comfortable circumstances, grief-filled experiences in waking life, are often manifestations of these phases. The astrologer takes on the important role of grief counsellor in supporting a person through such a phase.

Dreams often have a theme of disputed values between others and within the family. Such dreams seem to be significant in the lives of adolescents as they make the change from childhood to adulthood. Fear for future growth, the rites of passage from one status to another, are both components of the eighth house. Dreams can develop ritualistic themes, so that ceremonies that are familiar in waking life can feature, often with odd touches that seem to tap into the earlier foundation of such ceremonies, where ritual sacrifice and other cultural traditions touch on the more painful implications of such rites. At some level even the adult needs to be aware through dreams of those aspects of the inner child still undeveloped and experiencing pain and change as part of a natural process.

The Third and Ninth Houses

We associate the third house with language, with the mind and the way in which the individual has learned to use his communicative faculties, to function through the spoken word and through sense impressions imprinted on the developing mind. It also represents the development of physical mobility, manual dexterity and the individual's formative ideas about himself and his environment. If first steps, in a physical and intellectual sense, are accompanied by 'not safe' messages, the child's mind becomes conditioned to feel that exploration of a wider environment might also be 'not safe'. If those first steps, physical, verbal, manual and imaginative, are encouraged and applauded, then curiosity and the capacity to explore is enhanced. Much of the influence of those who teach the child comes not so much through the words spoken as through the way in which the developing child perceives what is being said. Body language is extremely influential in the third house – subliminal messages conveyed by adults in the first formative years hold just as much sway as the spoken messages.

If words say one thing and body language another, the child is tuned to absorb both messages and has to deal with the repercussions of such mixed messages later in life. Value put on education, on language and the development of skills by influential people in the child's environment will ultimately affect the individual's attitude towards communication and knowledge. For instance, I recall a recent outing with one of my daughters during which we were stunned to overhear a young mother say to her child, 'If you don't behave yourself, you'll have to go to school'! We were aghast at the implications and my daughter commented that she hoped she wouldn't be the one to teach the child.

Teachers – not necessarily professional ones – abound in the early learning environment, and their influence on attitudes and mental development, skills enhancement and curiosity about life, are all connected to the third house. Siblings and those people in the immediate environment during the growing years are part of the relationships experience too. During childhood, it is with siblings, or those who are surrogates for siblings, that one forms the first tentative relationships apart from those with parents, and it is here that the child practises his language, tests out thoughts and forms his ideas. Dreams can invoke unconscious sibling relationships and rivalries that might well surface in communication difficulties with others during adult waking life. Mercury and the element air are associated with the third house, and Jupiter's elemental fire with its polar opposite, the ninth house. The axis connects both personal and social levels of intellectual and environmental experience.

The Moon in the third house connects to the *learned* and educated ways of thinking, and educational institutions often applaud only the rational mind and those who conform. The dreamer then tends to seek out the truth of the dream in a rational and simplified way. However, there is often *hidden* and deeper significance in the apparent simplicity of the dream, as the potency of the ninth polarizes and draws the dreamer into the landscape of the imaginative. There may be a danger of simple images masking deeper truths and, conversely, of elaborate images masking simple and unpretentious truths. Third-house Moon dreams show the factual side of thinking that the dreamer has come to accept as the norm in daily life. This might extend to the superficialities that he accepts in dealings with people on a daily basis and his automatic acceptance of realities as expressed verbally by others. This is the house where he might need to question the truth of *learned ethics* and attitudes, and reorient towards what is his personal truth, perhaps in conflict with those expressed in the society in which he lives. Ethical, legal and religious matters are a part of the learning experience of the third house, particularly in childhood, and the third-house dream might encourage the dreamer to reassess his received ideas, or discard those imposed or imprinted by social expectations.

Relationship experiences of this house are with siblings, teachers and those in the early childhood environment who have influenced thinking from early days. Habitual mind-set patterns and the inhibiting factors of learned language, its colloquial limits and mannerisms – what we are allowed to say and what is deemed inappropriate in a verbal sense – are affected by cultural and environmental factors and are features of the third house. An example of a third-house moon dream is Kelly's blob dream, which was illustrated on p. 20. Third-house dreams enable the dreamer to articulate feelings and opinions that he might hide in worldly life, and can be quite surprising in that they reveal what he might unconsciously want to say to those around him. What he may avoid saying in actuality he can say freely in the dream! The dreamer might then see his inadequacies in communicating with others. Overcoming such blockages is made possible through dreaming, and what the dreamer might have come to believe about his own mental or communicative faculties through attitudes towards him in childhood, he can rework, realizing that those 'messages' have been wrongly interpreted by his developing intellect.

There is a latent mental fertility in the third house; intuitive, creative ideas and abstract perceptions, which may have been educated out of existence in life, are awaiting discovery in this house. Third-house dreams show us where we may be feeling unsettled. Alternatively, they may show where latent intellectual potential, unconditioned by rational education, seeks expression, and indicate how we might expand our mental pursuits through the opportunities for change and growth found in the ninth house. They also serve to illustrate and remind us of the encouraging messages from teachers, family and the learning environment that we have received and stored in the unconscious and not fully actuated in life.

The search to widen the scope of life experience is related to the ninth house and to the associated planet Jupiter. It correlates with higher education, law, religion, the higher mind, sophisticated communicative skills and mobility at its most extensive, and so extends the closed and 'safe' environment of the third house to distant places and cultures. It connects with the basic search for truth through religious exploration, the search for the meaning of life beyond the familiar. Without mental development and a widening of potentials through exploration and abstraction, one cannot conceive of anything over and above the ordinary. The idea of something beyond the present has to come before any exploratory moves, and so the ninth house finds its seeds in the third – its polar opposite. If the seeds have been sown in infertile ground, nothing grows in a ninth-house way.

Because the third house tends to lean towards the rational, left-brain patterns of thinking, the ninth is representative of the imaginative, right-brain function, so there is a natural flow between these houses, blocked only by conscious notions and attitudes. In the unconscious there is free passage between the two houses and so it is in dreams that the ninth house opens up and free flowering occurs for dreamers. When rational, logical and explicit thinking dictates life, the mind compensates by bringing dreams that open up all the possibilities present in ninth-house vistas. The most graphic and imaginative dreams can occur to compensate for a routine and overly analytical daily life.

The ninth-house dream brings to light the wider social environment and the desire to expand life, and orients us towards external personal growth and the search for the 'godlike' or numinous self. Meeting the self in a ninth-house dream can be an inspiring experience, for it is here that we can define our own potential. This polar axis represents the dreamer's capacity to grow from basic education and information to higher knowledge and abstract thought; from basic skills to artistry and from safe locations to unknown and exciting foreign territory. It implies possibilities for achieving intellectual, moral and social standing in conscious life, and represents the desire to transform restlessness into exploration and adventure. The dream may help to overcome fears of leaving the safety of known landscapes for the joy of adventure.

Early school experiences and blocks fixed in the mind during childhood are often features of ninth-house dreams, as the Moon directs light on to specific areas in waking life – personal, social, intellectual and environmental – in which the full panorama of possibilities is being denied, thus enabling the dreamer to identify the blocks and overcome them. The dream will focus on what might inhibit the dreamer from fully utilizing the urge to grow in an outer way and will encourage the self-confidence necessary to achieve such growth. Inner restlessness, opinions one may wish to express but cannot articulate, opinions expressed by others, siblings or relatives about one's mental capacities, all come under the spotlight.

The dreamer whose childhood is littered with put-downs from teachers, family and sibling relationships, comparisons with others and messages of being 'second best', may find all these surfacing in the ninth-house dream. Subliminal resentments or, alternatively, the awareness of the pleasures and joys expressed in childhood sibling relations feature, so dreams here can also connect to the delights experienced in childhood.

In accessing the higher mind, the dreamer accesses his own latent potential and suppressed intuition rises up from the unconscious in an active way so that the dreamer rarely wakes from such a dream without some sense of anticipation or excitement. This house is futuristic, it uses the springboard of the third house but can develop potential well beyond that promised in childhood, so that it represents further education, evolving philosophies and exploration of ethics and principles gained from outside the familiar confines of home. It projects the mind forward and promises progress in the broadest possible sense.

The Fourth and Tenth Houses

The axis of the fourth house and its polar opposite, the tenth, involves the Moon and Saturn – emotional and social imprints connecting the boundaries and conditioned values by which we experience security and warmth, and feelings of being loved and nurtured. Astrologically it is analogous with the parents, home and family security, discipline, the social background, and the shaping and lessons learned from socializing experiences that may be either comfortable or self-defeating. Astrologers view this axis as the parental axis, and indeed it can represent the parents but, at another level, the two houses connect the 'inner parent' and 'inner child'.

Psychologically it represents the capacity of the individual to nurture and care for their own emotional needs, as well as representing the nurturing he received in childhood, so dreams that are in either of these houses will touch on one's capacity to parent oneself. It is the area of life experience where an individual develops a sense of mature status, and is often expressed in establishing a career. This sense of maturity or vocation is encouraged in fourth-house life and opened up and developed in tenth-house life.

The fourth house represents the deepest conditioned emotional nature of the individual. It originates in personal family experience, in that of the extended family, in tribal roots and deeper still in the collective experience of nurturing, growth, fertility and death. Dreams will connect to the emotions in a very powerful way, for this is the Moon's house. It represents lost emotional memories, and those imprinted from racial, collective, tribal and family patterns.

The Moon is in a sense where it belongs, in the water element to which this house is connected. Its meaning here is as the root of all subjective experiences, so it will illuminate anything that may still be newly fertile, infantile, unevolved, growing or needing nurture. This house carries the seeds of future creative potential and so is immensely fertile. We find remnants of childhood in this house and those remnants may be comfortable or disturbing.

Through the fourth house we dream of the extent to which we might aspire in the tenth house. This is the emotional comfort zone, different to that of the second house, which represents physical and material comfort. Here comfort can be found in childlike dependencies. It is comparable with the kind of dependent relationship experienced in infancy on which we base our so-called security, but which, if not challenged, restricts growth and maturity.

Periodic withdrawal from society, retreat into the quietude of one's own soul to heal the wounds that occur in life, is healthy provided the individual is still able to come out and get back into the mainstream of life. The fourth house is the ultimate place of safety, an allegorical womb to which one can withdraw for periodic sustenance but in which one can become stuck, refusing to grow, forever sucking on the metaphorical breast of inaction, routine and protection. In dreams, this house represents those needs that require to be outgrown, feelings and emotions to which one clings for security. Many such motifs are not valid in adult life – they belong in the landscape of childhood, and one may see oneself as a child in fourth-house dreams reacting as a child and, as an adult, not like or willingly accept what is revealed of one's infantile responses.

There is a tendency, when consciously searching for answers to emotional dilemmas, to try deliberately to reach and bring out all buried matters, but the Moon here indicates that only that which arises *spontaneously* is valid. Some things may be best left buried and dreams are the most reliable way of determining how far we need to go in reworking emotional conditions. Being buried means accepting that there are some emotional and personal experiences we cannot consciously change, and so we resolve them, up to a point, through acceptance, while the soul deals with those matters that can be healed. It does so through dreaming. This house clings to the past; it is only by letting go of the fourth house and all its implications that one can reach the polar opposite house, the tenth, where the goal is maturity. Concomitant with maturity is worldly achievement and standing, respect and admiration in a social environment outside the safe confines of home.

Relationships along this axis are with parents, authority figures, mentors and role models in waking life, those to whom we pay respect – or detest because of their apparent power over us – and who, in reality, represent our own potential maturity. Saturn and its element earth are associated with the tenth house. Dreams illustrate how, through mastery of our dependencies in the fourth house, we might become such an authority and hence have dominion over our own objective world. In conscious life there are times when one may feel powerless, experience feelings of being unloved. Such self-defeating emotions become the fault of those in authority whose love one seeks, but who do not fulfil those needs. Those figures and images are aspects of the potential self at its most evolved. The fourth-house dream evokes feelings that encourage the dreamer to examine his own emotional sensors and defence mechanisms in some depth This is the house where one can seek out what one needs to nurture the *whole* self – the fountainhead of emotional well-being.

Earlier, on p. 41, we examined Michael's Santa dream as an example of a lunation phase dream. In that dream the new moon occurred in the fourth house. It might be a good time now to re-examine the imagery of that dream for its fourth-house implications. The dream presented images of Michael placing his daughter, who was alternatively Santa Claus, in a bath, to rebirth her. We can see both the images of the wounded inner child Michael and the potential 'authoritarian' Michael, interwoven in a dual image. That Michael's authoritarian side was in the image of a figure representing gifts and giving, at a celebratory time of faith, implies that his own authority is in his personal characteristics of innate generosity and faith. Michael was able to heal some facet of his inner child and bring the creative side of himself back to life. In the dream, he was phoning authorities outside himself, but was unable to complete the phone call. At the same time an assassin threatened to break through the transparent window, but Michael took control of the situation by reversing the dream and reclaiming his power.

Home, security, protection, creativity, authority and the child state are all matters that are central to the dream, along with habitual mechanisms of defensiveness and fear of loss. Positively, Michael reclaimed his authority, healed some aspect of his inner child, dealt with fear and was able then to reach out in worldly life and begin to write his play. In the fourth house we can discover the fruitfulness of our lives.

The tenth house represents the desire for prominence and status. Life experiences that give a sense of achievement, of fulfilled goals and of standing in the community all connect to the tenth house. Positively this gives the individual a mature standing, from which to perceive life in a holistic, secure and rightful position of fulfilment, to achieve the admiration of others and act as a mentor or guiding light to those less experienced.

This house represents the father figure or mother figure at its most encouraging. It is the most elevated of the houses in the mandala of the chart and as such represents all the laudable qualities of the individual, those qualities that put him in a position of being looked up to and respected for his wisdom and maturity. The tenth house represents the qualities of self-respect, based on love in the fourth and good social paradigms and flexible boundaries in which to grow. When the personality is not receiving due respect, or is unable to recognize self-respect but is dictatorial and manipulative, it is because of seeded insecurities in the fourth house. There is an inability to separate cherishing love from admiration and, through the tenth house, a seeking for love that seems lacking at an infantile level of the psyche.

The individual can misinterpret approval and admiration as love, and demand, not earn, what masquerades as love in relationships with people in the outside world. In this way, the tenth-house experience can manifest in a co-dependent way, when one seeks admiration to allay fear.

When the Moon is in the tenth house it highlights facets of achievement, worldly success and public acclaim. The tenth-house experience draws on the fourth house and has a deep-seated emotional attachment to areas of career and public recognition, or the search for approval based in the emotions, and hence is neither mature nor objective but tied to some immature habitual need. This tenth house is a house in which one might live inviolate, yet by polarity to the fourth house one is vulnerable. The deeply wounded soul often wants to prove it has no need of love, only admiration. The tenth-house dream will illuminate the hardened defence mechanisms which deny love at its most nurturing. While the adult in the tenth house can deny the emotional base of the fourth house they must also realize that their emotional base may inhibit them from progress.

Michael was to have another dream a few weeks later. This time the dream Moon was in the tenth house. He named it his 'tornado dream'. 'I was carrying a pile of books and a child. A tornado swept through the town, which was something like a film set. First I tried to hide under a bridge but it didn't feel safe; then I found an old shack and tried to get into it but the wind was strong and I realized I had to let go of either the books or the child in order to be safe. I decided to take my chances and hang on to both in the hope that we could survive together. Both the books and the child were swept from my arms, but I was not afraid. After the storm died down, I found the child in the shack, picking up the pages of the books that were littered around.'

The Moon in the tenth house draws attention to the two outer planets, Uranus and Neptune, and the north node in the meaning of the dream. This dream is highlighting Michael's capacity to stand out in a way that promotes him to a position of status once he can overcome obstacles in his life or pass through any barriers that might inhibit his progress. The Moon is, in a sense, directing him towards his true path through contact with the node, possibly highlighting ego issues to be overcome, and is also drawing attention to the transpersonal potentials of Uranus and Neptune.

Mercury in the second house of resourcefulness is in a trine aspect with the Moon and square to Pluto. The message is clear – something needs to be destroyed so that new life can emerge, and it concerns tenth-house matters as well as fundamental childhood themes in Michael's life. By polarity and through the trine between Moon and Mercury, it also involves some facet of the fourth house that may be restricting him, or is an emotional matter that needs attention so that Michael can apply his efforts to achieving standing and making his mark.

Michael reported that he had made a start on his play but it was not working out the way he had hoped. His works to date had centred on social and racial issues, and were quite serious and often contentious in content. He is of mixed-race descent and, like many young aboriginal people in

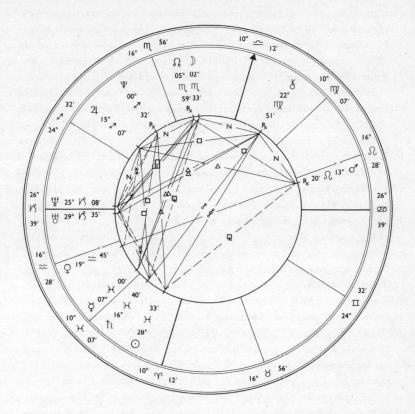

9. Michael's Tornado Dream (illustrating tenth-house dreaming)

Australia, is trying to fit in with social values imposed on his traditional heritage. He, like many in this situation, feels a deep longing to connect with his aboriginal cultural roots, yet is also aware of his Anglo-Saxon heritage. His dilemma is that he – and there are many like him – feels a need to choose between very different cultural origins and as a consequence has a confrontational attitude to an authority that is vested in the European system.

Through this dream, and the earlier dream, he came to the conclusion that he needed to change his attitude at one level and in waking life should abandon the style of writing in which he was secure and tackle something different. The message of the Moon–Mercury trine is one of creative imagination; both planets in the water element imply that Michael has a wealth of hidden resources that are only now beginning to surface. It also speaks of cultural and racial boundaries and a confusion that is being breached. He can indeed become notable by taking charge of his own creativity and being willing to take a risk.

We discussed how he might explore his creativity in a new way, and some months later, Michael reported that, despite having no faith in the system, he had applied for and, to his surprise, received a government arts grant. Together with a musician friend he had begun work on a theatrical piece that would get his social message across in a very different way.

Relationships experienced through tenth-house associations are mainly those of superiors or authority figures, encountered in job and career paths. In life these figures represent role models or people who can be of value on the journey. Those who are in positions of power over the individual also figure in the dream imagery, and any unworked insecurities about matters pertaining to the fourth house can become matters of importance in the search for standing in life. They often are represented by the people who seem to be the regulators of the system in conscious life – how one deals with the system in waking life is often a measure of the maturity of the psyche, and may be shown to us in the dream.

The Fifth and Eleventh Houses

The planetary connections with the axis of the fifth and eleventh houses are the Sun and Uranus – the identified cultural self and the unique and spiritual self lying beyond the boundaries of worldly reality. The axis represents what one identifies as the self in the world and the self to which one might aspire if one were not limited by the expectations of society. Negatively, it corresponds with the potential breakdown of identifiable standards by which the self measures its worth – the axis of crisis of reality or identity. The fifth house indicates a capacity to reach out in life and grasp all its fun-filled, joyous aspects, to take risks in relationships and in material ways, and to be aware of the 'I' or ego. This house is important since, by being the Sun's house, it is where the central sense of the individual self begins. Astrologically, it is easy to dismiss this house simply as the house of risk-taking, children, sport and love affairs, without looking at its deeper connotations. It is in the fifth house that we access the positive and the negative potential for identifying the self with the outside world and, by polarity, for identifying with our special place in the universe.

Howard Sasportas put it thus: 'We must remember that the Sun, although vitally central and important, is not the only Sun in the galaxy – it is just one of many. The words of a popular song remind us that "everybody is a star". Embedded deep in our psyches, and reverberating throughout the fifth house, is an innate desire to be recognized for our specialness.'[5] This is the house where through awareness of one's uniqueness one might feel isolated. Isolation is not necessarily a negative experience, for this house throws one back on the energy of self-reliance, separated from the polar opposite, the eleventh house of peer expectations and group activities. Sol means the sun and in the sol-itude of aloneness one might indeed tap into a sense of spiritual connectedness with the source, perfection or godliness within.

In dreams, the Moon in the fifth house seeks out those aspects of the self that are in need of clarification. Relationships assigned to this house are primarily those with children as creative projections of the self, with love 'affairs' and with ways in which one is willing to test one's self by questioning values instilled by parents in childhood. In highlighting this house the Moon encourages us to separate the self from the generational and peer structure of the eleventh house and stand alone and proud. It will indicate latent talents and creative abilities and, by focusing on the eleventh house, will show where individuality is being affected by peer expectation and where one is being influenced and affected by the collective at large.

Fifth-house love connects with loving of self and being lovable, and with affairs of the heart from which the individual gains a measure of self worth. Romance, rather than commitment, is a fifth-house experience and sex mainly a matter of experimentation and exploration. Here the dreamer may experience his own sexuality or inhibitions, and be able to discover the urges that he might joyfully express in uninhibited sex in waking life. To love the self enables one to offer that love to others and enter into committed relationships; thus love affairs are a way of testing our capacity to love before committing ourselves to a partnership. This is the house of flirting, of testing out and taking risks before commitment; dreams may show those with whom we flirt and play, and so may reveal developing relationships. It is a house where the dream content is often enjoyable, where, since the Moon comes close to the site of the Sun and its seminal creativity, one experiences delight in becoming who one is.

Dreams often link to waking matters that are current in the life of the dreamer, and highlight the generative or productive nature of his worldly life. The Moon may light those aspects of self that are in poor condition, are being overshadowed or defeated by pessimism, or affected by group expectations with which the individual cannot identify. Dreams can lift and enrich the psyche, eliminating gloom – one can dream for fun or to remember how to have fun, as illustrated by the example on p. 67, my duck dream. All creative processes funnel through this house and include such activities as hobbies, recreation, creative and artistic endeavours, and talents that are ready to be exploited and so become productive in life. The challenges one meets through activities such as sport and other competitive pursuits which enable one to shine in some way are all matters that arise in this house. The dream Moon will focus on areas in the collectivity of the eleventh that might benefit from the dreamer's creative endeavours. There may be intuitive inspiration in such dreams, as the Moon sends a light into the eleventh house and singles out progressive, futuristic and humanistic motifs, and relationships that can either benefit from or be of benefit to the dreamer.

The eleventh house represents attitudes to peers and those waking activities which connect the individual to the human condition at large. How one fits in with peer groups depends on the capacity of the individual to be both separate and unique and yet connected. The fifth-house/eleventh-house axis is a paradox of detachment and attachment. In the fifth house we desire to be unique and special, yet we seek confirmation of this in the eleventh by searching for others in the world on the same wavelength.

Uranus rules the eleventh house and so can draw the individual away from his core identity to seek a different identity, even beyond the birth family. The connection Uranus makes with the idea of crisis might imply the potential for crisis of identity along this axis. We see this acted out in life, as young people, seeking to find a sense of their individual identities, express the desire to be different, yet, though breaking away from the norms of their parents, conform to quite rigid standards expressed by their peers and friends! This implies that being different is a dynamic step to discovery of a higher self and seeks confirmation and actuation outside of the established identity. Risks have to be taken to find what might be appropriate and thus the fifth-house/eleventh-house axis represents taking a creative risk in breaking away from ego identity in a search for progress.

The eleventh house represents the house of inventiveness, where the creative urges of the fifth are being taken out into the world and made manifest. We call this house, in traditional astrology, the house of hopes and wishes and the house of humanitarian concerns. Hopes and wishes for a better life for humanity lift the individual beyond his personal ego-centred consciousness and activities and into the wider collectivity of politics, race and group consciousness. Dreams may bring deep-seated prejudices and attitudes to light that one might deny in waking life. The Moon illustrates that, while the individual does indeed live out his life as an individual, he maintains an inexorable link with others in a social system. Dreamers may discover where they are not interacting with others, where the urge to be special in the fifth house is divorcing them from the common ideal of betterment for all.

To seek a better life successfully often means a reappraisal of personal desires, and an eleventh-house dream asks that we examine how one might benefit from peers or offer something of benefit to the collective. In this house the Moon illuminates the many collective issues in worldly life that ultimately affect the fifth-house individual self: the collective chip on the shoulder that might inhibit personal creative expression; collective conditions in outer life that might offer opportunities to shine; collective and peer expectations that might rigidly fix the individual into a pattern of conforming to social expectations – these are all matters brought to the dreamer's attention. Relationships and love through the eleventh house connect to friendships and relationships which are not rooted in intimacy, emotion or co-dependency, yet afford one approbation and a sense of kinship. Peers, children and students that the individual teaches either by example or by profession, and those who have affected his life but are unrelated by blood, are all part of the eleventh-house experience.

The urge for universal connectedness through an undemanding love of humanity is part of the house experience. In this regard eleventh-house dreams might highlight where one might rush in to tilt at windmills, to offer one's self without first ascertaining the worthiness of those who are to receive it. We instinctively seek social connection, and although we are born with an essential sense of belonging within a family, there is still an urge to find the 'ideal' family, one that implies equality rather than hierarchical structures. Every person is drawn, through the eleventh house, to find undemanding relationships that are beyond the boundaries of family and often extraneous to socially 'acceptable' norms, so here one might find those associations that are deemed 'unsuitable' by parents. The dreams of adolescents in this regard are significant when the Moon is in this house, as they touch on matters of what is right and what is wrong. Sexual matters arise, too, often in adolescence when there may be ambivalence over sexual orientation.

The Sixth and Twelfth Houses

The sixth house is the house of welfare. It is the house where a process occurs to maintain psychic health, physical health and well-being, both for the individual and in his concerns for the welfare of others. It represents the tasks and work one undertakes in daily life to maintain well-being and a useful life, and implies pulling it all together so that life is working smoothly and harmoniously.

At a deeper level this house shows the tasks we need to undertake to sustain psychic health. It lies at a point where self must give way to include others, and self-ish interests must sometimes be set aside to accommodate the needs and interests of others. This is the preparation site for intimacy with others, the house of serious courtship following from the fifth house of flirtation and leading to the seventh of bonding. This can apply to working or business relationships too. Matters of relationships in this house include the feasible aspects of intimacy and the unconscious work that needs doing to enter successfully into intimacy.

The Moon encourages the dreamer to sort through the practical realities of partnership and determine what aspects of his own ego needs he might have to sacrifice to enter fully into the exchange required in a bonding relationship. The subconscious realities and workable components of partnerships show clearly, and the messages may highlight what is not working in intimate relationships.

The axis links bodily and psychological health and the waking-life activities undertaken to maintain psychosomatic health. When the Moon is in the sixth house it may highlight danger to health. Illness, whether of a physical, emotional or psychic nature, always threatens well-being and wholeness. Particularly, if the Moon is in earth, it is well to examine the dream for indications affecting physical health and other material matters. Polarity with the twelfth house can highlight chronic or deep-seated illness and psychological traps into which we might fall. It also connects to the self-sacrificing nature or the sense of martyrdom that can accompany a poorly conditioned ego structure. Through polarity the dream will show where the dreamer may be forfeiting the right to self-determination, being dominated by the services he performs for others. The sixth-house dream may be quite specific in pointing out what is not working, what resentful attitudes and emotions are blocking smooth performance in life and may need to be reworked so that the holistic balance is re-established. We get great insight into how well we are doing in life's mandala through the sixth house.

The planetary connections are Mercury and Neptune. Service, work, self-sacrifice and the routine matters that affect daily life all arise along this axis. The sixth house is where the psyche is concerned with integration of the useful, viable and practical facets of life. The twelfth is where the psyche deals with dissolution of the useless and unviable, and so dreams might connect to the unconscious decisions that need formulating in waking life regarding specific projects, relationships and goals. Most questions and answers about life sit on a fine line between the rational mind, represented by Mercury, and the intuitive sixth sense, represented by Neptune. The sixth house is where one might seek answers to conscious problems, to work things out. Tuning in to the intuitive twelfth house enables the dreamer to tap into deep and seemingly mystical sources, sources which run through one's own unconscious, giving answers to conscious dilemmas. In the twelfth house matters of ego are not relevant and so these answers are not affected by the ego or by waking situations but are objective and impartial.

Relationships with co-workers, with current daily companions or those who depend on the offices of the dreamer all connect with the sixth house – also our relationships with childhood companions and, in particular, the emotional contribution siblings have made to our sense of well-being. It is here that old wounds can emerge and seek healing. Resolution to long-held resentments through sibling rivalry feature in the sixth-house dream and the dreamer may be surprised at how deep such battle scars may be, and how they are expressed in his current attitudes and relationships.

The twelfth-house experience is one of accessing subconscious blessings and also problems hidden away in the unconscious. Hidden, that is, where they affect worldly life and psychic balance. The escape mechanisms by which one might avoid confronting facts and the pipedreams that replace real achievement come to the dreamer's attention through the Moon in this house. One may see sides of the self that are paradoxically both holy and profane. Ego is at its most distant in this house, while spirit and soul are shown in their truth. The dream may take on mystical proportions not experienced in any other house. This is the sacred site of Neptune. Here, through the dream experience, there is potential bliss and the dreamer may be shown ways to achieve blessedness. This is a house where one can express emotions freely and this will be part of the dream imagery and content.

Many twelfth-house dreams are simply healing dreams that require nothing more than that the dreamer enjoy the feelings invoked. However, not all dreams carry a guarantee of pleasure and bliss; some may indicate those subliminal conditions which block holistic development. Polarity with the sixth house enables the dreamer to review his feeling function so that in waking life he can express emotion more potently and in harmony with the inner spirit. He experiences and learns how to express unconditional love without self-sacrifice. This polarity will also indicate the levels at which we may feel ensnared, seduced by ideologies, people, addictions or habitual attitudes of dread that inhibit full participation in life's wonders.

When the Moon's light percolates through this house, it brings out what might be imprisoned in the dark, unresolved fears and experiences that plague the psyche, often emanating from very early pre-language memories or even experiences *in utero* imprinted on the psyche of the child before birth. The dream gives an opportunity to confront the unfamiliar and complex fears and phobias that plague conscious life, leaving the dreamer insecure and apprehensive. In focusing light directly on the sixth house, the Moon shows how one may become free from the entanglement of phobic behaviours and become more effective in mainstream living. Relationships of the twelfth house are personified by those spiritual mentors or guru figures in whose teachings one might seek the truth. Dreams also highlight the unconscious influences of mentors to whom one has emotional attachment, those persons of prominence in life who might influence our social and political opinions and ideals through example. One should treat dreams flavoured by the twelfth house with great reverence, as by them we are able to see clearly into the truth of things.

7

Aspects – Synthesis of Self

Vision is the art of seeing things invisible.
Jonathan Swift

ASPECTS

There can be no relationship with life unless there is touching and exchange, and the same principle applies in astrology. Planets interact and essentially form relationships by touching, connecting and exchanging energies according to their individual principles. The varying transit cycles of the planets means that, at any given time, there is a variety of 'relationships' forming and breaking up. The 'lunation process' examines the waxing and waning cycles of the Moon as it orbits earth and so forms geometric angles with the Sun that we call 'aspects'. The same principle applies where any faster-moving planet forms waxing and waning aspects with slower-moving ones, and astrologers study the constant interplay of these angular relationships in their attempts to understand the cyclic nature of life.

The angular relationships formed as planets cycle vary according to the degrees of separation, and the aspects so formed describe the manner of the relationship and the exchange within it. We define the calibre of relationships between planets by measuring the geometric angles between them as they unfold in their cyclic motions. Each aspect defines the quality of the relationship according to the angle between planets within the 360° circle. Astrology has come to understand that specific angular relationships correlate with specific 'types' of interrelationship.

We call some angular relationships 'hard' aspects. This is because the quality of the relationship between the two planets is a strong, noticeable exchange, pointed, defined and challenging. In the chart, hard aspects between planets are those which indicate a potential difficulty, tension or crisis, or indicate a possible turning-point that can be clearly marked in the dream chart. Hard aspects range from short-term predicaments experienced in waking life to long-term psychic predicaments that have been constellated in the unconscious. Hard aspects mark differentiated parts of the whole self in the unconscious at the time of the dream; they allow us to recognize and actively participate in making conscious changes.

Other aspects we call 'soft', where relationships between the planets are more in accord and there is an easy exchange of the meaning that is embedded in the planets' symbolism – a more subtle and non-confronting interchange and relationship. Soft aspects are more healing and pleasant; they imply confidence and compatibility between the planets, reassuring and bringing pleasant images in the dreams, effectively assuring the dreamer that relationships between specific parts of the whole are being reconciled.

Aspects used in dream-chart work include the conjunction, square, opposition, sesquisquare, trine, sextile, quincunx, quintile, septile and novile, and the dream chart should be drawn up to include these aspects. The geometric calculation of aspects involves dividing the 360° circle into specific divisions. For example, the square aspect divides the circle into four parts, the angles being 90°. However, it is only for a brief time that aspects are likely to be *exactly* 90°, and so we make allowance in our calculations that are called 'orbs of allowance' – a few degrees either side of the exact measurement. Each astrologer tends to define the orbs according to what works best for him or her. For this reason, the orbs used in the charts in this book are those that work for me and should be used as a guideline, and other astrologers should use orbs that are in accord with their own personal preference. However, it is worth remembering that the closer the aspect, the more acute its meaning, making the dream purposeful rather than vague in its intent. In this book dream charts and natal charts have the following orbs of allowance: 8° for the conjunction, square, opposition and trine; 6° for the sextile; 4° for the quincunx, quintile and sesquisquare; and 1° for the septile and novile. When comparing the dream chart with the natal chart, these allowances are halved. The reason for this will be explained when synastry is explored.

Aspects that need to be examined first are those between the Moon and the planets, and those formed by Mercury to the planets. Aspects will also form between other planets, but unless they are connected to either the Moon or Mercury, they have no direct import on the dream but indicate the climate in which the dream occurs.

The Conjunction (0°) ☌

The conjunction creates a 'marriage' between the principles of the planets. When two planets in their different cycles come together in the same space they are not just side by side, but are absorbing each other's principles in such a way that they become inseparable for a brief time. This is an intense and powerful exchange when the diverse meaning of each planet flows into and around the other. This process of cross-fertilization creates new meaning. In essence it is a 'new-moon' phase, according to the planets involved, when new potentials can arise out of the melding of the separate planetary potencies.

Some conjunctions make a smoother blend, as the symbolism of the planets is essentially more compatible; with others the conjunction is an uneasy and prickly meld. Because of this variable, the planets involved need careful consideration. The principles of the planets can create a fusing that is highly creative and redolent of pleasure, sensitivity and cooperation, or one that is ruthless and driving and potentially explosive, like a time bomb waiting to go off! The conjunction implies either integration or splitting of some aspect of the self, so that even if the planets involved indicate strife, the conjunction offers a way to bring something out into the open.

The Opposition (180°) ☍

The opposition is a powerful and direct statement, especially in a dream chart which involves the Moon or Mercury in this aspect. When the Moon opposes any planet it is shining a direct light on to the meaning embodied in the planet. There is no doubting the Moon's intent to bring the planet into high focus. The purpose of the dream centres on the meaning of that planet, experienced in the polarity of the houses.

An opposition between planets may create a relationship of direct confrontation and conflict between the principles of the planets, but there is also polarity between them, in a similar way to the polarity between houses that are opposite each other. There is a two-way flow with potential for compromise and settlement as well as discord and division. Planets are face to face, and so there can arise a dynamic of one principle imposing over the other, especially if their meaning is paradoxical. Conversely, the principles can complement each other and meet in compromising fashion as one principle makes way for the other. This is the paradox of the opposition. The Sun and Moon, Mars and Venus, Jupiter and Saturn are all paradoxical pairs and, when opposing, are capable of separation and disharmony as well as integration and compromise. Oppositions that involve personal planets and transpersonal planets are perhaps the most difficult to deal with, as they involve facets of conditioned reality and potential surreality.

When Mercury opposes a planet a message is described clearly. Similarly the Moon brings great clarity into the reason for and meaning of the dream, straight from the heart of the planet's meaning to the heart of the dreamer. Geoffrey's lovely dream illustrates the feeling and spiritual nature of the twelfth house. Geoffrey dreamed, 'I was standing on the deck of an old sailing-ship. There were twelve other people, all in flowing robes of indeterminate colour. Each carried a stoppered glass bottle. As each in turn made eye contact with me they took the stoppers from the bottles. An elderly man came forward and said to them, "Everything is alright now," and one by one, like genii, they each entered their bottle. The old man took me by the hand and led me to the wheel of the ship, smiled and disappeared into his own bottle. I was left alone with twelve bottles in a neat row pointing to the prow of the ship. I awoke feeling extremely happy and sang all day.'

The Moon opposes Jupiter in the sixth house – growth, upliftment, transcendence to the higher self and self-improvement are all embedded in the dream purpose. The opposition polarizes and highlights health matters, tasks, work and unconscious ideals or fears that are part of Geoffrey's efforts in getting his life to work smoothly. Mercury transmits a message from Chiron, by a trine aspect, with a secondary aspect to Venus. Wisdom, together with an assurance of worthiness and love, compose a message in which there is no tension. Mercury is also conjunct the north node, implying that finding the true path or vocation is involved in the dream. The dream shows that Geoffrey is not stressed, particularly in matters to do with health, work and the orderliness of his life – a simple message with a direct point! A few years ago, Geoffrey had left a seminary, where he was training for the priesthood. He does not have any doubts about his decision. A few weeks before the dream he had opened a natural therapy clinic and was just a little concerned that things had gone *too* well. Activities at the clinic were accelerating at a great pace, and he loved the work and felt he was growing spiritually too. (The Moon at the time of the dream was exactly conjunct his natal Jupiter.) He determined that the purpose of the dream was to show him that his conscious and unconscious life was indeed on the right track. He was also awaiting the results of a regular health check-up, for a condition that had recurred periodically in his life, and the following day received the

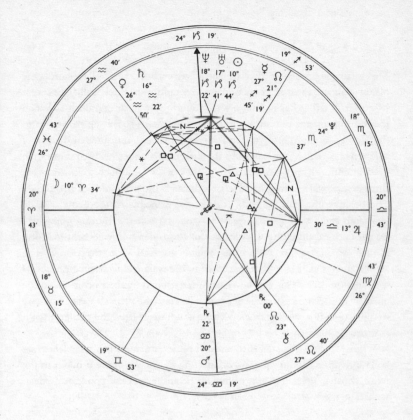

10. Geoffrey's Bottle Dream (illustrating the opposition aspect)

information that all tests were clear and that he could extend the period before his next check-up.

The Square (90°) □

The square is an aspect that can be filled with unresolved tension. One planet in square to another encounters a metaphorical brick wall. To express its power, it either has to find a way around the wall or demolish it. When the Moon is in square to a planet, the planet seems to put up resistance to the Moon's intent to bring it into focus and so the significance of the planet is in tension. The Moon's light in the dream chart does nothing more than draw attention to the nature of the planet or to some facet of waking life that is tense and is being experienced through the principles of the planet. The positive implications embedded in the principle of the planet can be lost from sight with a square aspect – they represent a turning-point or a point of critical shift. One should take into consideration whether the Moon is in a waxing square or waning square in relation to the planet. The significance is similar to that discussed in the waxing and waning phases of the lunation cycle. This can be visually determined by their positions in the chart by house: if the Moon is in a house 'before' the planet, in anticlockwise motion, then it is waning in its cycle; if in a house 'after' the planet, then it is waxing.

When Mercury is in square to another planet, the message has a deliberate and motivating flavour. Matters connecting to the planet are brought to the mind, those matters that are needing to be addressed and consciously dealt with. The message is clear-cut and powerful.

The Sesquisquare (135°) ⌑

The sesquisquare resonates to lengthier, unresolved and ongoing dilemmas – an insidious aspect, implying that as one crisis is resolved, another is in the making. For this reason the meaning locked in a sesquisquare can be one of the more difficult ones to find in the dream chart. The aspect corresponds to themes of worry and anxiety, problems not confronted, desire for growth denied. These correspondences all leave a sense of discontent and it is this dissatisfaction that can become the theme of the dream.

When the Moon aspects a planet in this way, it is drawing attention to something that is only partially resolved. This can be a dangerous aspect, and it implies that a problem that the dreamer might have believed solved could rise again. The sesquisquare clarifies the themes in life experience most in need of ongoing work: waking dilemmas or dilemmas of personal growth that are inhibited and repressed, only to beleaguer and gnaw at the dreamer. When Mercury is in this aspect, the message is of long-unresolved worry and contains imagery that harks back to an almost masochistic refusal to let go.

The Quincunx (150°) ⊼

The quincunx is formed at a point between the complacency of the 120° trine aspect and the challenging 180° opposition aspect – and can be imagined swinging like a pendulum between them. The aspect illustrates both how one might need to deal with matters head on and how one can tend to take the easy way out. It implies the need for confrontation followed by adjustment at all levels of expression. Great care needs to be taken to understand the implications of this aspect when it is formed between the Moon and a planet, or between Mercury and a planet.

This aspect most often appears accompanied by other more direct aspects, when it implies that an unconscious shift of focus has occurred, but sometimes it can appear as the more potent aspect. Then health is one of the areas that manifest its power, in cases where sickness is unconsciously used as a means to escape some problem or circumstance. The toxic nature of this aspect is such that the person is then trapped by his own escape mechanisms, a victim of his own illness. The dream where it appears might require the dream worker to attempt, with tact and diplomacy, to uncover any psychosomatic illness in the life of the dreamer. Similarly, it might appear in dreams where dreamers have been long-time victims of circumstances other than health that appear to be beyond their control, and the dream may illustrate that determined activity in worldly life can help to overcome such circumstances.

The Trine (120°) △

The trine creates an effortless flow of energy between the planets forming the aspect. Dreams with strong trines are pleasant and healing dreams. When the Moon forms a trine to a planet in the dream chart, it draws attention to the more pleasant, growth-oriented and positive attributes of the planet.

This enables the dreamer to access healing potentials, even when he is under stress in his waking life.

When the trine combines with hard aspects to other planets there is an opportunity for resolving some dilemma by integrating the positive attributes of the planet with the trine, but the hard aspect might overshadow the trine. The planet might even point a way to a solution for some waking dilemma. Gloria's cream-cake dream, examined on p. 96, illustrates how the Moon square to Saturn served to highlight family tensions. However, the Moon was also in trine to Venus, and so there was in effect an infusion of love and sound value judgement that implied that Gloria could solve the problem because she loved her husband and valued the relationship.

Venus is the planet most concerned with striking a balance and so it was that Gloria was able to bring the dynamic of love, harmony and balance into the discussion of the situation and work out a compromise with her husband. With the trine aspect, little conscious action is involved; the aspect seems to operate at a subliminal level, reinforcing and reassuring the dreamer, so they may wake feeling happy and take the feeling into their consciousness. When Mercury is in trine aspect to a planet it brings a reassuring and healing message, tapping in to the positive attributes of the planet, so that even a planet with such powerfully negative potentials as Saturn or Pluto might 'send' creative and reassuring messages through the trine relationship with Mercury.

The Sextile (60°) ✶

This aspect connects planets in a relationship that is functioning smoothly, enjoyable, successful and viable. It is common to find the Moon or Mercury forming a soft sextile aspect as well as hard aspects. As with any soft aspect, the hard aspects can overshadow the sextile so that it operates at a more subtle level, acting in a compensatory way. When there are hard aspects to contend with in the dream chart and, by reflection, in waking life, sextiles imply quiet confidence in the meaning embedded in the planet. If the hard aspects are confrontational and demanding, and life experience reflects the same, there is, through the sextiles in the dream chart, an undertone which implies that despite difficulties, something else is functioning, some facet of the psyche is operating in the way it should, compensating for difficulties.

When the Moon's only aspect is a sextile to other planets, it draws attention to soul and to the individuation process which is working towards a cohesive whole. Thus the feeling is one of inner strength and confidence, reassurance in matters relating to the planet. When Mercury is only aspecting by sextile its message is one of confidence that something is going according to plan. This may well refer to some project in waking life that is partly completed, to a relationship newly formed and at the stage of developing more meaning, or to inner work that has been undertaken by the dreamer specifically in order to improve and develop personal traits.

The Septile (51.4°) S

This aspect divides the circle into seven and has spiritual and psychic overtones as well as shadow undertones. It connects with the gestalt fields of the outer planets, beyond the seven visible planets and the threshold of Saturn, and so to the supernatural planets of the collective. With a 1° orb in the dream chart, the septile can indicate a meeting of souls in a transpersonal way. This aspect arises when a dreamer has dreamed of an actual person in his life, only to find that the other person has had a similar dream. In the dream chart, it is as though there is a deeper message, a telepathy, and if the dream involves people, it is worth looking at the prophetic or telepathic portion of the dream. If the Moon is involved in the septile, it may be that the person known to the dreamer is part of the reason for dreaming and is in effect speaking to the dreamer in a telepathic way. Many people claim to be able to leave their bodies and travel the 'astral plane' – and if this does happen, the dream might describe the contacts made at such a level. This is the aspect of inspiration at its most exquisite, and the dreamer might well receive a spiritual message that can be brought into fruitful and creative reality.

The darker side of the septile can be sinister. If septiles occur regularly in dream charts, and involve the same planets, there could be intrusion into the dream, and the dreamer may identify the person in the dream with someone who in worldly life is in some way manipulating them. Dreamers might experience a feeling of being taken over during sleep by such a person and there is an element then of paranoia if the dreamer succumbs to the fear of being manipulated. Positively, this can occur when the dreamer is not making use of the inspirational ideas and signals received from the spiritual dimension. Other aspects, whether they are hard or soft, together with the planets involved will be a clear indication of the positivity or negativity of such repeated patterns.

The Novile (40°) N

In dreams the novile speaks of an ideal, or of a seeking for perfection. It can clarify what the hero self would aspire to become, but can also indicate an ideal that is in no way attainable under the conditions of conscious life. When the novile appears between the Moon or Mercury and other planets it should be viewed as offering the opportunity to bring something to perfection, given the circumstances that are described by the other aspects. Like other less direct aspects, it can be overlooked as the more potent aspects take precedence, so it will operate at a subliminal level. In some ways this aspect implies a level of maturing, of something reaching ideal form, and so can be very useful in the dreams where decision is called for.

Typically, Anna's resurrection dream has a novile between the Moon and Jupiter and also one between Mercury and Saturn. Underpinning the dream and her consequent actions, Anna has, without being aware of it, achieved a level of maturity at a point in her life when she hovers between child and adult status and many of her decisions will be judged against the norms of society. Thus her actions can be seen, not as the impulsive actions of an impetuous child but as the intuitive actions of the emerging adult. The novile can be described then as an intuitive exchange between the planets involved. I have also found this aspect in the dream charts of those who believe they have received a divine message and take the message literally. Should a dreamer decide that they have received a calling, it is important to examine the chart and current outer planet transits to ensure that any message produces decisions that are feasible. (Had Anna decided that she should drop her studies and go to Africa on a mission of mercy, the novile would be unproductive, given her lack of skills. That she may do so later in her life is a matter for the future, as this aspect might indeed be a calling.) Thus this aspect can be most fruitful and progressive in the search for perfection, if it is found together with aspects that keep it within bounds of possibility, given the life conditions of the dreamer.

The Quintile (72°) Q

This aspect connects to the principles of both the inner self and the conscious identity, and can be most creative in a dream chart. Using a 1° orb, if the Moon is involved in a quintile with other planets, then the dream will effectively empower the dreamer to grow and develop a sense of their own stature, to identify something special in the planet's creative meaning that is exclusive to them and which is capable of bringing great joy to their waking life. It brings awareness of gifts and talents, creative abilities that are developing and coming to maturity, and will make the maturation process effortless and enjoyable. Even if there is tension in the dream, at some level there is creativity under way and the dreamer may experience a sense of anticipation that evokes feelings of confidence.

When Mercury is involved in a quintile, the planet is sending a message that can be most valuable in coming to some solution in any conscious dilemma implied by the dream chart. The message might tell the dreamer of undiscovered skills and capabilities that can be brought to the situation and used to work towards a fruitful and joyful conclusion. This is the aspect that creates reassurance and even a little self-congratulation, as it reflects the self in its creative efforts to improve and grow.

RETROGRADE MOTION

At times, from the geocentric perspective, the planets appear to travel in reverse motion, and this has the effect of extending the time frame. We call this retrograde motion. In effect, the planet backtracks over ground that has already been transited and, because of the relative positions of earth, planet and Sun, it may make three and sometimes five passes over the same point in the circle we call the zodiac and so repeat the aspect it is making to a natal planet.[1] We allow an orb of 1° in determining its proximity or exactitude in making the aspect, so at times the transiting planet will appear to be beyond the scope of the orb, but, if it turns retrograde or direct during the time frame under review, it will return to transit within that orb again. It is more effective then to take the entire time frame into consideration when looking at transits and view the exact periods as times when awareness of the transits' ramification is at its greatest.

If a planet is retrograde in the dream chart, it illustrates a dynamic phase in its passage across the zodiac. The phenomenon of retrograde only occurs due to the earth's position in orbit around the Sun, and so it aligns with worldly activity and expectation. The dream chart in a sense transcends worldly matters and so a planet retrograde will be symbolically more inclined to express a deeper meaning and significance as the paradigms of worldly 'reality' fall away. Retrograde implies introspection, and so one might find a deeper significance as the dream chart is the introspected picture of the dreamer's world – a doubling of introspection, in a way. Retrograde, in technical terms, does imply that, in transits to the natal chart, it may have already aspected a planet and may be now in a position where the dreamer is attempting to make sense of the situations that have arisen when the first aspect was formed. If the retrograde planet in the dream chart is one that is involved in major transits to the natal chart, it represents a phase during which potent dreaming can occur, with specific reference to the life situation of the dreamer, and the dreams are likely to be highly significant in dealing with such a situation. The dreamer is more inclined towards introspection at this time.

The dream chart captures all the planets' transits at the time of the dream and so it is likely that Mercury will be demonstrating retrograde motion in some dream charts. Mercury's aspects to other, slower-moving planets, when in direct motion, will re-form if Mercury turns retrograde and metaphorically goes over the same ground again. As mentioned, the core meaning of Mercury does not change through the phenomenon of retrograde, but, like outer planets in retrograde, will tend more to introspection. Retrograde motion by Mercury implies that this planet is acting in the capacity of Psychopompos – the guide to the soul in Greek mythology – and in doing so accesses and brings potential healing to old wounds. It has already formed an aspect and it is very likely that a significant dream has already occurred.

Retrograde Mercury will bring the same message from the same planet as before, but the more occulted facets of the message might emerge in the dream. The language will tend to be more symbolic. What may have been brought to notice in a dream at the direct stage is often better comprehended at the retrograde as the dream takes imagery from the earlier dream and reshapes it. In this way dreamers can be helped to make the connections. As Mercury turns direct again, the symbolism might be clarified even more. Recording dreams over a period will reveal the incidence of backtracking.

There are two possibilities with Mercury retrograde dreaming. The first is that retrograde dreaming will connect to unresolved themes that may have arisen about three months earlier when it was in direct motion and will come to completion at the next direct phase. (The planet involved in the aspect should be checked to see if it is involved in potent outer-planet transits to the natal chart and what timing is involved.) The second likelihood is that the regular retrograde mechanics link each retrograde cycle.

In this case, another process, connecting retrograde dream to retrograde dream, brings dreaming that has a source constellated in the shadow part of the psyche, in suppressed childhood experiences or in unresolved complexes, and might involve aspects to different planets each time, or different aspects to the same planet. Such dreams will re-address themes time and again and are often only accessible during Mercury retrograde periods. Unresolved messages may continue a theme for years, only emerging during retrograde cycles, the dream seeming to skip from one retrograde phase to the next and implicitly linking to the earlier dreams. Matters harking back to other retrograde phases will be invoked as each new cycle comes into being; 'lost chords' re-form into a harmony that has potential to heal in a broader sweep.

An example of a dream with retrograde Mercury illustrates this capacity to tap into old, stored, childhood messages that have lain dormant for years. The dreamer was a man in his early fifties who was, to say the least, a reluctant client. He came to see me out of 'curiosity', at the prompting of a friend who felt he might gain something from an astrological consultation. He was recently divorced for the third time and held a high position in the political arena. He mentioned in passing a dream he had dreamed that morning. I offered to explore the dream with him, as a way to break through his defensive and belligerent attitude.

'In this dream I was adult but acted like a child. I was in a city but decided to leave my parents as I saw a circus and wanted to watch the show. I needed to step over a long hose to get to the circus and was very afraid to step over it. It seemed very dark and rainy on the other side. I stood there for a while until I saw there were adults at the other side so I stepped over it and found myself in a carnival, near an old derelict warehouse. I went into the warehouse and found a puppy. It was crying and I picked it up. I hid in the warehouse with the puppy but it whimpered and gave us away. A clown came along and grabbed the puppy and hurt it, nearly killing it. My parents came and I yelled at them but they said there was no puppy. I tried to cry but the tears wouldn't come. My parents told me to be brave and not look at the puppy. I thought it strange as they claimed they didn't see it. It's odd, but when I woke up, I felt something had actually been sorted out, but I felt angry and upset.'

This dream is notable in that six planets plus the nodes are all retrograde. The Moon is in the tenth house, making a direct opposition to Chiron in the fourth, a square to both Pluto in the seventh and Mars in the first house. It also forms trine aspects to Jupiter in the sixth and Sun and Mercury in the second. The Moon is drawing attention to several facets of Anthony's life, his nature and his relationships. It is doing so both through the stressful aspects to the planets in the seventh- and first-house axis, and through the healing aspects to the planets in the second and sixth houses. Furthermore, and most significantly, the Moon shines a direct light – by opposition to Chiron in the fourth house – on his emotional self, rooted in the safe environment of his childhood. In the tenth house, the Moon highlights Anthony's standing in the world, his attainments and mature experience, in which conscious prestige, achievement and worldly authority are underpinned by emotional well-being or limited by emotional barriers. Here we are supposed to be adult, not infantile, and this is reflected in Anthony's dream as he sees himself 'adult but acting like a child'.

There is enormous discomfort in this tenth-house dream in that it captures Anthony's naïve feelings, tunes in to the childlike fears and early pain through Chiron and, with the hard aspects made by the Moon in this chart, those feelings that account for anger and extreme violence. Anthony's defence mechanisms are down and he feels exposed in this dream to feelings he has denied in the search for status and acclaim in political life. Long-repressed material is brought to light by the Moon in opposition to Chiron. It isolates woundedness, the capacity to wound and the early childhood rage still deeply embedded in Anthony's psyche and now brought to light as Mercury becomes doubly introspective. The Moon has entered water from air – effectively shifting from thinking to feeling modes of expression; this too is symbolized in the dream as 'dark and rainy on the other side'.

Retrograde Mercury is aspected by the Moon so the message is a Moon message. The connection to the fourth house, to the feeling nature, is linked by a healing trine. Mercury is also in conjunction to the Sun, so the message is from the central self – in the sign that is naturally ruled by the Moon and connects to the fourth house. Mercury is also in a trine aspect to Jupiter and Saturn. Both these planets connect to Anthony's social and political training, his urge to grow and mature within a framework of established ethics and boundaries. Mercury makes no hard aspects, so the message is one of healing, a simple, harmonious message of love, a closed retrograde circuit in the water element, subjective and deeply emotional, that can flood Anthony with love, acceptance, reconciliation, forgiveness and self-healing.

There is a distinct connection with a childhood incident that gives some insight into the wounded child Anthony. In dialogue, we explored the idea of a circus as a mandala, or sacred space representing the unconscious. That

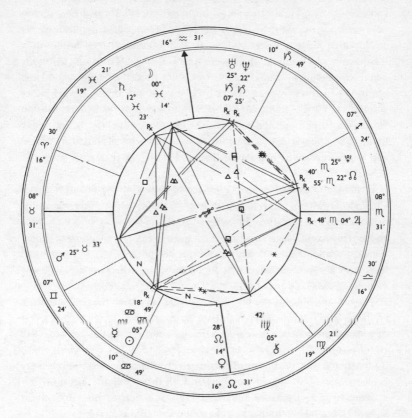

11. Anthony's Puppy Dream (illustrating retrograde planets)

Anthony felt afraid to step over the boundary was very apparent in his life and attitude to anything he viewed as 'hocus-pocus'. I asked him what a hose on the ground might represent to him. He recalled that, during his childhood in wartime Britain, his family had to evacuate their home when their district was bombed; there were fires and chaos. The young Anthony had to run beside his father and at one point needed to step over a large fire hose which was moving under pressure. He was afraid, but his father was carrying another child and told Anthony to keep moving. In the confusion he was left behind – in the dark, afraid to step over the hose. It was many hours before he was reunited with his family and he recalled that they were very angry because he had stayed behind. He was angry, too, at being left behind.

Examination of this incident connects it closely to the dream imagery. Childhood was not easy for Anthony – a large family, poverty and a determination to rise above his origins. Anthony is a man who is irritable and aggressive, unable to show affection and extremely demanding of others – in consultation he was determined to get his money's worth! He has had three marriages and several extramarital affairs, and in each marriage he was violent towards his partner.

The moon highlights the fury and rage that have been part of Anthony's life since he was small, and which have motivated him to reach high levels of political prominence, career and financial success, to the applause and confirmation of his peers – yet this same rage has left him emotionally dysfunctional and unable to maintain relationships. He was initially very belligerent and scathing of astrology and 'all that feminine-side stuff' but softened as time passed. I felt that there was a cry for help in such an attitude, since he had bothered to keep the appointment, at least.

Together, we explored and he learned about the 'accidental' nature of deeply entrenched woundedness, the anger that he had carried with him, not necessarily because of the hose incident but perhaps because of other childhood circumstances when his feelings were not considered. He began to see how he had suppressed his feeling nature. This dream did put him in touch with his own inner child – the disconsolate Anthony, who was 'abandoned' by parents, and who uses rage to deny basic feelings. This insight was to have a remarkable effect on Anthony. He has since completed a programme of exploring alternatives to violence, has learned to face his rage and grief and acknowledge them, and, with the support of a new partner, is learning how to express his loving nature, in a 'feminine' way and not deny his softer side by, in the words of his parent, being 'brave' in a masculine way, but reconnect with instincts for compassion and love. The dream enabled him both to forgive and to be better able to reach an understanding of himself and the interactions within his relationships, and so move forward. Subsequent dreams show remarkable progress and he is now as passionately for inner work as he once was against it.

Not all retrograde Mercury dreams will access stored memory in such a specific fashion, but may access stored sense impressions, which might invoke memory, reworking them into imagery. The facts may not fit the soul's perception so precisely as it has in this example, but the feelings component will mirror those that may have been felt at the time. In Anthony's case, Mercury accessed a real but forgotten incident, triggered by the symbolism of the hose and its personal meaning to Anthony. (This is not his real name and, to protect his identity, his natal chart is not available for publication.) Outer planet transits to the natal chart at the time were: transiting Saturn conjunct the IC and transiting the fourth house, trine natal Chiron novile natal Moon and septile natal Venus; transiting Uranus square natal Saturn; transiting Chiron conjunct the MC and transiting the tenth house, to aspect by trine to Venus, Mars and Jupiter over the following months; transiting Pluto trine natal Sun.

OUTER PLANETS' TRANSITS TO THE NATAL CHART

People usually turn to astrology when they are experiencing uncomfortable predicaments and difficult phases in life. Astrologers note the way in which the outer planets' transits synchronize with life's phases and they have, by experience, come to understand the outer manifestations and inner personality changes that take place at such times. When counselling a client, astrologers commonly use the technique of defining the symbolism embedded in transits of the outer planets and other methods of projecting the planets' positions into the future, from the astrological 'tool-bag' of methods.

The natal chart does not imply a static quality. Outer planet transits in particular mark regular phases of development in life and so can manifest outwardly in quite predictable ways. The unconscious manifestations are at risk of being relegated to a back-seat position as we address predicaments experienced in day-to-day life and try to cope with them. Both in our own lives and in those of our clients we tend to attend to matters at an outer level and are less inclined to pursue the inner transitions and developments that are taking place in line with those outer experiences. The value of working with dreams is that it enables us to see how inner personality changes can ultimately manifest in beneficial consciousness shifts.

Transits do not 'cause' events to happen, because they are 'in the sky' – it is the inner, unconscious phase cycles of psychic development that instigate outer shifts in consciousness, and these are represented by the transits of the planets in symbolic form. For example, the planet Pluto transiting through the second house, in conjunction with Venus, which might oppose Saturn natally, does not come along and *force* the person into debt and bankruptcy – it is the inner Pluto that *motivates* an urge to make enormous changes in value paradigms. The client who is experiencing such a dilemma is not always open to understanding that at a psychic level they, or their soul, require such experience to grow. Such a client takes little consolation in being told that at an unconscious level they may become a better person because of the experience. In conscious life, we use the rational mind to make sense of life experience, but the answers lie in and emanate from the unconscious. We might encourage introspection, but the person who is depressed by his experiences will tend to dwell only on the impediments and suffering, and he may avoid, or be unable to access, the healing that is available.

Introspection is furthest from conscious mind when we seek to deal with the ramifications of a given life situation, but it occurs every night in sleep as the ego attachment to worldly situations falls away and the scope of the inner Pluto and other planetary symbols is freed. Working with dreams enables the astrologer and his client to take the healing power of the unconscious into daily life and approach the plight from a different perspective. Throughout life, graphic dreaming occurs as the psyche tries to make sense of outside experiences. Dreams embody psychic renaissance at some level that can be brought to consciousness.

The dream chart illustrates a point in time when the planets are so placed as to create a symbolic dramatization of the link between the unconscious and the conscious. We are able to see how the unconscious is attempting to make changes manifest and how solutions can come from the deeper and wiser and more experienced dimensions of self. The dream points to a specific moment – during an outer planet phase – and causes an inner metamorphosis. We are never the same after a dream – something always transmutes. As mentioned, the dream springs from the spontaneous action of the unconscious. It is synchronistic with the positions of the planets at the time. The dream experience is then *at the motivation of the unconscious* and happens during specific phases of planetary transits, the conditions under which the dream occurs.

Setting up a chart for the brief insight into the unfolding of life's process is a powerful way of divining soul's purpose. The dream chart is a chart of unconscious reaction to outer experiences and of the soul's independent activity at the time, and reveals the essence of symbolic life. The dream chart *can stand alone*, and has in the first instance been examined without reference to the natal chart. Nevertheless, there is even more to be understood if it is synthesized with the natal chart.

Outer planet transits to the natal chart occur all the time, as the planets orbit the Sun and symbolically travel the mandala of the horoscope. As they do so, they make aspects with the positions of planets in the natal chart. These contacts last through periods of time corresponding to the time that it takes the planets to complete a full cycle. The slower outer planet contacts are made for extended times and so have come to be understood as major developmental phases in life and psychic experience. The natal chart represents a moment in time that becomes a lifetime's awareness of conscious life. Using the technique of synastry, correlating the dream chart and the natal chart, we are in effect, presented with a conjugating of conscious and unconscious. In this we are able to perceive the individuation process in action. We see a glimpse of this process at a given point in the journey through the dream.

Outer planet transits are generally experienced in three phases: as the planet first passes over a sensitive point, as it retrogrades back over that point and again as it resumes direct motion. We are faced with a constellation of energies working within a phase cycle similar to those that other people will experience. Each individual experiences these transits in their own way, and yet they are a part of the collective experience. The time for the planet's passage varies according to the planet that is involved. This also applies to retrograde timing, which often extends the time taken to complete the transit.

It is during the first direct passage of an outer planet that we most often have conscious experiences that highlight particular dilemmas. During the retrograde period, we can become more introspective, assimilating and digesting those experiences, being empowered at this time to investigate the 'soul's intent'. Dreaming can occur at any stage, but the more fruitful dreams seem to occur at this retrograde stage. As the planet again turns direct we might become more aware of the need to take action and resolve matters, but the vibrations of the experiences and the planets' transits stay with us, unconsciously, for a long time. The natal chart and current outer planets' transits to the natal planets give an important focus on the dream's purpose. Dreams do not simply occur, out of context with conscious life and activity; indeed, it is that activity that alerts the unconscious to the need for dreaming, and often at the time of a dream the dreamer is experiencing potent and noticeable transits.

Outer planets' 'hits' – contacts by aspect with natal planets – extend over approximately two years, but the momentum begins to build up long before those aspects are within the 1° orb and it reverberates for some time afterwards. The time frame can extend to a period of up to five years as the individual unconsciously pre-empts the changes that occur over the period and consciously integrates them. When a transiting 'hit' is no longer within orb, the effects of the transit do not simply end – resolution and active integration takes much longer.

To take account of this, when working on the synastry of the dream chart with the natal chart, it is advisable to use a larger orb than that traditionally used in examination of transits to the natal chart. The unconscious is aware long before the apparent manifestation of outer planet transits. By using larger orbs than those commonly used in transit work, and smaller than those used in natal charting, we can examine phases both before and after they appear in conscious activity.

As previously mentioned, I halve the orbs used in setting up the dream chart and natal chart. This allows one to see the outer planets' transits which have recently left natal contacts and those that are still developing. Any aspect differential that is greater than 1° will imply an aspect that has already happened or will happen shortly. If the aspect is 'applying', then it is entering and will come within a 1° orb quite soon and might warn of impending problems. Those that are 'separating' are those that have already occurred, and their manifestations are being worked on in life. Effectively this extends the time frame of the transit experience to encompass an unconscious pre-emptive stage and a conscious reconciliation stage.

INNER PLANETS' TRANSITS TO
THE NATAL CHART

At the same time as the outer planets' transits synchronize with major events and themes in life, the dreamer is experiencing transits of the inner planets and the luminaries. Inner planets are those from the Sun out to Jupiter and include the nodes. The transits of these faster-moving planets are hardly noticeable in consciousness because, compared with the transits of outer planets, their 'hits' last only days or, even allowing for retrograde phases, at the most months. The brief passage of the Sun, Mercury, Venus, Mars, Jupiter and especially the Moon are unobserved during the activities that surround conscious life, yet the Moon continues to collect and absorb all the consequences of conscious activity. Jupiter will make an aspect to a natal planet for about two weeks, while Mercury, Venus and the Sun will aspect for at most two days. Mars too will make contact for two to three days, while the Moon will transit for hours only.

But in the dark of night, as consciousness is suspended, we get an opportunity to cross the threshold to inner life and experience something that might ultimately change our life experience. When working with dreams, particularly in an ongoing capacity, it is not essential, but certainly advisable where possible, to examine the natal chart and the current outer planet transits to natal planets for a broad insight into the dreamer's conscious processes. One should examine them over a cycle of about two to four years to obtain a framework and then examine the inner planets' transits for more detail, to home in, so to speak, on the dream within that framework. Comparing the dream chart with the natal chart brings details to light within the 'big picture' – a microcosmic insight into the process – at a moment in the life of that cycle. Such insight might well change the outcome of the phase. A synastry grid, similar to that used in the study of relationships where one person's planets form aspects of those of a second person, is a useful astrological tool to employ in this context to record visually the outer planets' transits and the personal planets' transits with natal planets at the time of the dream. To do this, I consistently place the individual's natal chart in the 'across' position and the dream chart in the 'down' position.

Aspects between dream planets and natal planets bring awareness of the natal potential embedded in the planets' meanings that is reinforced, conditioned and confirmed by worldly experience. Hard aspects made to natal planets are powerful contacts. Together with natal propensity they challenge the dreamer to examine the conditioned and habitual ways in which he may express those archetypes in his daily life and so learn something of his own response mechanisms through the dream.

For example, the dream Moon may not be making an aspect to dream Venus in the dream chart, but if the dream Moon squares natal Venus, then, in addition to the message of the dream chart, the dreamer might be challenged to explore their Venus nature and, through the dream, learn more about their personal value system and affections, and the way in which they are expressed in waking life. Similarly, soft aspects will not challenge but heal and gently change the way in which the dreamer expresses those planetary meanings. If the dream Venus is in trine to natal Saturn, balance, love and healing energy become absorbed into the Saturn nature and this has the effect of modifying the conscious expression of Saturn. The infusion of meaning comes, not from the singular and conditioned expression of meaning, but from the scope and amplitude of collective meaning. This is how dreams heal at another level of psychic experience.

When the personal dream planets do make contact with a natal planet, it is worth examining whether that planet is involved in a longer phase cycle, and integrating the meaning of the contact when counselling the client. To sum up, the transits of outer planets can affect life in a broad sweep of major growth and change, trouble and dilemma, and inner planets can affect life on a day-to-day basis within the context of the broad experience. The following examples will give a brief idea of how the inner dream planets might be effective in the life of the dreamer – the dream worker should explore the possibilities with the dreamer. The definitive *Planets in Transit*, by Robert Hand,[2] is a very useful adjunct to understanding the specifics.

Dream Sun to Natal Planets

The transit of the Sun forms aspects with other planets for only a day or two. When the Sun contacts natal planets there is a symbolic exchange as the Sun vitalizes and infuses the planet with creative energy and takes some of the meaning embedded in the planet, identifies with it and brings it back into consciousness. As the dreamer wakes he can do so with a deeper understanding of those particular personal energies that are unaffected by expectation and conditioning. The passive nature of the dreamer's ego, or 'I', meets the psychic entities dwelling in the unconscious in a manner that corresponds to the aspect formed and then the 'I' returns with a gift or challenge to their own psychic potential. Often these planets are involved in the broader passage of outer planet transits. So any planet the Sun contacts will bring a deeper, more particular understanding of that planet's meaning, an understanding which becomes part of the dreamer's nature, thus empowering them to identify and integrate its truth into conscious life.

Dream Moon to Natal Planets

The contacts made with natal planets by the Moon are extremely brief. Only in the dream will the aspect form, applying a few hours before and separating in the hours which follow. The Moon not only illuminates the dream purpose but also nurtures through contact with natal planets, and so touches those facets of the dreamer's nature that are in need of sustenance and care. The Moon acts to bring instant relief, so that the power of the planetary archetype is sustained and renewed. Through its contact, those facets of personality that have been neglected are succoured. The Moon's contact with other planets will evoke feelings according to their principles. Energy is restored at an emotional level and the dreamer is able to bring feelings into consciousness. These contacts can be a useful indicator to the dream worker of the emotive state of the dreamer, especially during dialogue, and the dreamer can be encouraged to express his feelings.

Dream Mercury to Natal Planets

Mercury in contact with natal planets enables conscious thought to be given to natal propensities as an added outcome of dreaming. It touches on the meaning of the planet in an intellectual way so that the principles of the planet may be better understood and articulated in waking life. It brings the principles of that natal planet in rational focus and renders them productive, since the dreamer can examine the natal potential of the planet's meaning, speak or think about their natal inclination and learn something additional to the dream in an academic, impersonal and emotionally non-threatening way. The way in which the dreamer articulates the dream, the words written or spoken, will be affected by the natal planet aspected by Mercury. If the dreamer has forgotten some detail of the dream, then dialogue about the natal planet can often stimulate recall. If the planet is an outer planet involved in the broader transits phase, and hence projected into life experience, then

Mercury enables the dreamer to take particular notice of the message in the dream and apply it to any current situation, maybe even use it in discussion with those people who are involved in the problem. Mercury is often retrograde and if this is the case, the planet it aspects should be investigated for internalized motifs – it is as though Mercury has the capacity to reach even deeper into the meaning of the planet and bring some aspect of it to the surface that is worthy of lengthier discussion. For example, a retrograde Mercury may be in conjunction with natal Mars and Mars does not appear to be involved in the dream. Whether natal Mars is involved in outer planet transits of a difficult nature or not, the dream creates an appropriate time to review or discuss Mars-related motifs, as the retrograde nature of Mercury brings something to the surface that has been simmering but to date has not been actuated. This could pre-empt negative action to the benefit of the dreamer, even if it is as simple as a warning that he may be subject to unproductive temper outbursts at the time. It also enables the dreamer to discuss and express frustration or anger in a rational and controlled way.

Dream Venus to Natal Planets

Venus' contacts bring peace, love and healing to the planets. It touches them with love, with compassionate understanding, and so brings potential pleasure and joy to the planet. The person who experiences little love in conscious life may experience the infusion of a sense of self-worth and love in dreams, and if the lack of loving is constellated in the way he experiences that particular planet, Venus' touch can do much to redress the balance. Its touch is exquisite and brings strong feelings to the surface. Hurtful experiences that are attached to the meaning of the planet can be remedied. If Venus has been represented in life by relationships which have harmed the dreamer in some way, then it can bring the opportunity for forgiveness. If value paradigms and self-worth are affected by the planet, the Venus contact might encourage a review of the evaluating measures the dreamer uses in waking life. If the planet is an outer planet and is involved in an ongoing theme, Venus contacts bring a point in the phase when negotiations can take place or when the dreamer might re-evaluate his situation in a positive way. Venus is the least likely planet to be retrograde in a dream chart, but when this occurs, the Venus nature reaches deep into the meaning of the natal planet and touches it in a healthy and compassionate way. It will enter into the core meaning of the planet and invoke only those positive attributes that are embedded in that meaning. In dialogue with the dreamer, there is value in examining the positive nature of the planet, so that the dreamer is able to recognize his own positive and fruitful potentials.

Dream Mars to Natal Planets

Mars, like the Sun, is connected to consciousness through the means by which one achieves goals. It enables one to confront and excise poisonous conditions and take action to make creative changes happen. Mars encourages one to survive and thrive at a conscious level, so it will inspire, motivate and confront the planets it touches, challenging static conditions in those planets to awaken to revitalized action. Quite often the Mars message is the one that is remembered more clearly than other messages, and it invokes action and the desire to do something quickly about whatever dilemma might be indicated in the dream. The dreamer often wakes feeling angry, or excited and energized, and very occasionally takes action in an inappropriate way. Venus in the chart is an indicator of the balance and equalizing force behind any action, and dialogue with the dreamer will enable the dreamworker to ensure that action is not too impulsive. If the planet is an outer planet involved in major transits, then Mars might indicate that action needs to be taken or might enable the dreamer to express his anger at some facet of the transit. One might be able to counsel the dreamer to find appropriate ways to express Mars' energy, either by directing anger in an appropriate manner or by setting defined goals and using the energy as a tool to achieve them. Mars turns retrograde approximately every two years and when it does so, depending on the natal propensity and on its contacts with natal planets, things can seem to be out of control. When Mars appears retrograde in the dream chart, it may, because of the mechanics of the retrograde phenomenon, be in opposition to the Sun. If this occurs, then the dreamer can express feelings of panic, deep-seated anguish or rage. Aspects to other planets should be examined carefully, as they will indicate the source of such feelings and offer the opportunity to excise the pain.

Dream Jupiter to Natal Planets

Jupiter touches the planets with the potential to grow, to become numinous and amplified. Depending how close the aspect is to being exact, the effects may manifest for several days. It is during this period that the dreamer brings something of the planet's meaning into consciousness and can learn much about himself in the process. This is likely to be a valuable lesson. This contact will amplify all the positive facets of the planet's import but may also distend and distort some of its meaning out of proportion. It will bring knowledge and wisdom to some facet of the dreamer's personality, and inspire and uplift anything that has become depressed or inactive. Positive energies that have fallen into disuse can bloom again. The planet's action, like that of Mars, is to rework something in the unconscious and bring it out so that it can be integrated into conscious life. Care needs to be taken in dialogue with the dreamer, for he may exaggerate his capacity to deal with current situations, particularly if Jupiter is in a soft aspect, implying ease. However, the dreamer can be encouraged to adopt a more positive and optimistic attitude if the planet is involved in major transits. Jupiter marks, in its transit, phases of growth in a twelve years' cycle, so in aspecting a natal planet indicates a stage in that growth cycle. It is worth also checking the phase it makes to its own natal position, in the same way that one defines the lunation cycle. For example, if transiting (dream) Jupiter, in addition to forming an aspect with a natal planet, is conjunct its own natal position, then a whole new cycle of growth is about to begin, and the dreamer should have this explained to him. Ethical dilemmas can be the reason for the contact, and if legal matters are part of the waking experience, the nature of the aspect can indicate the possible success or failure of legal actions. Retrograde Jupiter brings the possibility of a recurrence of the dream, or a similar dream, within weeks, when opportunities for resolution may occur or the dream may be clarified or confirmed.

Dream Chiron to Natal Planets

Chiron in contact with a natal planet will give insight into the fundamental nature of that planet; it will tell the dreamer something about the planet that is instinctive and embedded in the core meaning of the planet. There is a lesson to be learned somewhere in this contact and the lesson might be a very useful one if the planet is involved in outer planets' transits. There is an element of prophecy in Chiron contacts and so the dream may well have a message concerning the future. Chiron heals through knowledge and so dreamers may find they wish to understand more about their own nature through exploration of the planet's meaning. If the planet is one that has been experienced at the wounded level of the psyche, then Chiron may be instrumental in bringing such matters to the surface for conscious healing. When Chiron is potent in aspect to a natal planet, the dreamer is often unaware that they have information or knowledge of the planet's meaning. It is a very healing experience for the dreamer to find they already have answers and wisdom embedded in their psyche and counselling can reinforce and uphold this fact.

Saturn, Uranus, Neptune and Pluto, the transpersonal planets, in aspects to natal planets, describe the current life phase of the dreamer and should be viewed in the same way as they are viewed in regular transits.

8

Dream Astrology – towards Wholeness

Dreams are faithful interpreters of our inclinations; but there is an art required to sort and understand them.

Montaigne

USING A SYNASTRY GRID

As mentioned, using a synastry grid is a graphic way to see transits – both those of the fast-moving inner planets and those of the slow-moving outer planets – and their contacts at the time of the dream. The dream chart shows the transits current at the time of dreaming and the following example will illustrate the use of the grid.

Marie's exorcist dream occurred six months after her noose dream (p. 45). At the time, she was experiencing a Pluto transit in opposition to her Sun as a phase cycle in her life – there are dramatic changes taking place, both consciously and unconsciously. Pluto is retrograde and so is heading back to pass over the same point that occurred in the earlier dream. The dynamics of the transits are becoming internalized and need to be worked through introspectively and thereby integrated at an unconscious level. Pluto is also in sesquisquare to Uranus and in square to the north node. Marie is still involved in the extensive Pluto transit phase that coincided with the break-down of her marriage and the aftermath.

At an inner level, she had been resistant to change, but now experiences a more introspective phase of the cycle when her dreams may be more acceptable. Both transiting Uranus and Neptune are square her natal Neptune, challenging her tendency to self-deception. Saturn separates from a square to her Sun and is direct, so its implications are that she must integrate and accept loss as part of the reconciliation process. In general, Marie is at a stage in her life when there is loss and anguish, a need to let go of the past and move forward. Her identity is being transformed and a transformation of

	☽	☉	☿	♀	♂	♃	♄	♅	♆	♇	⚷	☊	As	Mc
☽		△ 0A24									⊼ 0S05			
☉	✶ 2S33		☌ 3A53					✶ 0S57		△ 0S24			✶ 1S12	
☿											✶ 1S46			
♀		0S26	N 0A38	⊼ 0S47	☍ 3A01				□ 1S28		N 0A28			△ 2A16
♂		□ 2A12		□ 2A31	□ 2A06									
♃		⊼ 1A29			⊼ 1A36	☌ 2S38								✶ 1S53
♄		□ 2S30									☌ 3S01			
♅									□ 2A45					
♆									□ 1A43	⊼ 1A58				
♇		☍ 2S09							□ 1S57		□ 1S38			
⚷			□ 1S08						✶ 1A59	☌ 1A44				
☊	□ 2A40					0S10			⊼ 1A04				□ 1A19	
As									☍ 0A44	△ 0A29				
Mc									□ 2A25					

12. Marie's Exorcist Dream (down) to Marie's Natal Chart

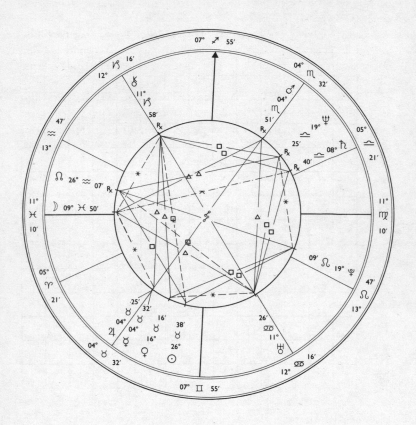

13. Marie's Natal Chart

her future is promised once the shift is complete and the psychological changes recognized and incorporated into her life.

Examining the inner planets occurring during the dream finds the Moon in trine to her natal Sun, so some facet of her personal identity is being nourished in a loving way. This is highly significant as it eases and heals the conscious image of self. The Moon in this aspect has an enormous restorative effect. Contacts between the luminaries are a key to the process of individuation. When the dream Moon and natal Sun form a soft aspect, that aspect takes on a subtle authority for healing, as it links the unconscious and conscious across the threshold, with ease and clarity. The mitigating energies of the unconscious and the conscious are integrated without effort. The Sun is conjunct her natal Venus, revitalizing her values and self-appreciation. In bringing this revitalization into consciousness, Marie wakes with a better sense of her worth. The Sun is also trine Chiron and so helps Marie identify her wise side and gain insight into her instinctive nature.

Mercury is in sextile to the north node and while it makes only this aspect, it is as though Mercury is gently pushing Marie in the direction of her true path and does not do so in an intellectual way but in a way that is consistent with her natal node in Sagittarius – intuitive rather than rational. This becomes a motif for discussion during consultation.

Venus is septile the natal Sun – spiritual healing from beyond the confines of her physical self is very effective in bringing love and renewal to her. This might be deemed a 'guardian angel' aspect, for it implies love from an etheric source that needs no rational explanation. Pointing out such an aspect to a dreamer brings a lot of benefit. Venus is novile natal Venus – she is inspired and can find within herself an ideal worthy of being sought. It enables her to know her own true value – to herself. Venus is in opposition to Saturn – Marie receives an infusion of comfort that breaches the boundaries and cuts straight to the heart of negative Saturn and all that it implies in Marie's life.

At the same time, Venus and Saturn together can create a real sense of peace and harmony – of feeling that one is on the right track and one's values are correct, and this aspect is important as it encourages Marie to test her own boundaries and self-limiting attitudes, at the same time as ensuring her that the framework in which she can live a good life is still intact. Venus separating sesquisquare to natal Pluto implies that she has been reluctant to let go of certain power themes, but through the action of Venus might be able to re-evaluate and heal any residual rage.

Mars is square to natal Mercury, Mars and Jupiter, and injects a sense of purpose into the dream. There is anger rising that might be able to be expressed verbally, judiciously and decisively. This aspect made Marie very aware of her internalized anger. Jupiter is in conjunction with Saturn and empowers Marie to define her ethical, moral and social activities, to work in consciousness to transcend the limiting and defeating patterns that are occurring. These are all powerful ways in which this dream might enable Marie to draw something from the unconscious that can bring worthwhile changes, in line with the events in her life. They are all matters for dialogue and represent potent ways for Marie to make progress in self-development and hence individuation.

Within the context of current life experiences, the dreamworker uses the dream as a way to counsel a client, to understand more deeply the processes of psychic or personal life – to determine the reason for dreaming as part of the transformation occurring. It can be reassuring to know, through dreams, that even though we may experience devastating loss, feel emotionally bankrupted or grief-stricken, deep down rebuilding and reconciliation of the psyche is taking place. It can also be challenging, in waking from dreams, to face those suppressed and denied energies, and maybe bring some truth into the open. In Marie's case, the dream is a message that empowers Marie to learn much of value about herself and her current situation, and realize that an inner process is returning her to more wholeness of being.

This was the first time I had heard from Marie after her noose dream. 'Throughout the dream there is a woman, dressed in white, with her eyes closed and a red mark like a fence over her forehead and eyes, floating in the background. Strangers approached me and gave me odd looks, and then turned me round to look at my back, almost as if they expected to see a notice or joke sign pinned on me. I had to climb a steep snowy track to a house and my job was to check milk vats so that I could fill them, but they were never empty. Little animals with pointed noses and sharp teeth attack me each time I have to go and check them, and I can only fight them off with a shovel. Each time I hit them their noses become flatter. I entered a room and there was a couch with a lid. Under the lid was a large lizard. It was friendly, but had no arms to hold me. I went to an old woman's house, high on a hill, which was a slippery climb and offered her red gloves. She was thrilled. She was on a ladder and I stepped on the rungs so that it would sink into the ground, rung by rung, and so she could come down towards me. The sleeping woman was there too, floating around, on my right. There was me, the old woman in front, the sleeping woman to the right. I woke with tears in my eyes but decided not to cry. I really do feel that something was exorcized, some evil was banished.'

The Moon is in the sixth house, in earth. It lights up the dynamic of getting her life in order, of the sacrifices she may have made for others, so creating unhealthy circumstances in her life, both physically and psychologically. There are hard aspects connecting the Moon in quincunx to Saturn in the eleventh and Mercury in the first, forming a yod. These aspects suggest an urging for adjustment, a reconcilement of energies, so that she can detoxify aspects of her life's journey and set about the practical task of getting her life functioning. The earth element suggests that the work is to be done at a realistic, practical and physical level. The sixth is the house where the process occurs consciously and unconsciously to achieve and maintain psychic and physical well-being. The Moon highlights the work that Marie must tackle, the tasks she must do to regain or restore a sense of equilibrium and wholeness.

In relationships, this dream highlights the viable aspects of her intimate relationship. Here she is challenged to sort out the authentic and viable aspects of this relationship and separate them from her personal wishes, fantasies or desires. Relationships with co-workers, work and health environment are all sixth-house relationships and the quincunx to Saturn highlights groups and friendships. There is a trine aspect to Uranus and Neptune on the mid-heaven which illuminates her capacity for mature change. Habits and routine emotional response mechanisms, sacrifices made 'on automatic' are brought to her attention.

The Moon's polarity with the twelfth house is focused on the martyred side of Marie, where we find Venus, not aspected by the Moon, but there by implication. It represents Marie's personal value paradigms, imprisoned, hidden in the landscape of fantasy. She may still be holding on to her image of what love should be, instead of taking a realistic view of the way things are. In doing so she undermines her own self-esteem and sacrifices her values. Mercury is in the first house and in square to Uranus and Neptune, so that the significance of those planets' meanings is a potent one. It also squares Mars, so it is bringing quite a complex message that implies a call for direct action to make changes. The message ties to the conditioned axis of the fourth and tenth houses — the child and the adult Marie.

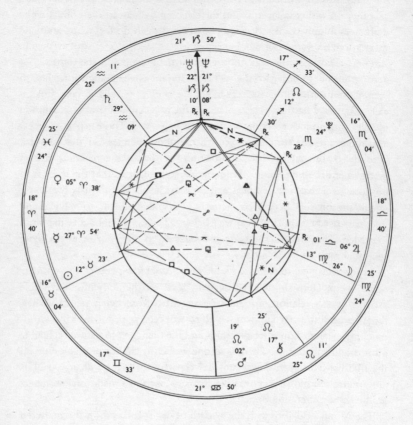

14. Marie's Exorcist Dream (illustrating inner planet synastry)

When several planets are tied to Mercury in this way, all have a say; there is collusion taking place with Mercury as arbiter or negotiator. Mars wants initiation, blood-letting, to effect a curative result and does so from the position of the immature and dependent Marie. There is a sense of awakening and a re-seeding of her own power to take action, but also the warning that her emotional state is rather childlike and she may not understand how to express her desire to initiate action.

Uranus and Neptune want structural change, for Marie to take a new direction and seek mature authority over her emotional dependences, thus making mental and spiritual progress. All aspects are hard aspects and may be difficult, but they are very motivating and the message is clear. Because Uranus and Neptune are transpersonal planets, the message is brought into personal consciousness through Mars. This dream may well be a turning-point.

Mercury's first-house position indicates that the dream will stay in Marie's conscious memory. The dream is dreamed for the purpose of resolving practical problems in Marie's life. The quincunx between Moon and Mercury is a difficult pendulum between thinking and feeling. Marie is challenged to confront and adjust her mental attitudes and feelings. It is pointed out clearly in the dream that feelings are toxic to the mind at this time. She is challenged to separate the two, to take a stand so that health can be restored.

In the synastry, perhaps most significance is the restorative aspect of the Moon and natal Sun. The dream is a turning-point for Marie. Through dialogue with the symbols and examination of the charts, we were to uncover a growing sense of excitement as Marie woke up from her inactive state. Although very much saddened by the dream, she experienced it as a catharsis, a painful but valuable experience. Unconsciously, she was changed by the dream; consciously, she felt empowered, yet still anxious. The dream was a catalyst to making practical changes and several dreams and months later her life changes began to unfold in a new direction. She began to put many practical plans in place to ease the transformation that was a current part of her journey. Today, almost four years later, she has a new profession, a new relationship and a new location. She still talks about this dream.

Recording dreams is a wonderful way to see life unfolding in the unconscious, as periodic transit phases connect with outer events and developments. Gloria recorded all her dreams as a way of studying their unconscious meaning so that she could make conscious changes during a very difficult and crisis-ridden time in her life. During a particular phase, she experienced the following outer planets' transits:

Transiting ♇ ☍ Natal ☉ ☿ ☊ MC
Transiting ♇ △ Natal ☽ ♄
Transiting ♇ ♂ Natal ♃
Transiting ♅ △ Natal ☉ ☿ ☊ MC
Transiting ♆ △ Natal ☉ ☿ ☊ MC
Transiting ♄ △ Natal ⚷ for most of the period.

Gloria, who we have met before, is an only child, married with three adult daughters, the breadwinner of the family; they have suffered financial setbacks and still struggle to make ends meet. She is a gifted teacher, a deep thinker and somewhat frustrated by material concerns in her desire for professional and academic growth. The manifestation of these transits are expressed by problems with her in-laws, her parents' deteriorating health, her husband's inability to work because of failing sight, and difficulties with the authorities over obtaining a disability pension and medical support for him because of her earnings. But to obtain such support, she would need to earn less money and consequently could not expand in her profession. She began her professional life as a primary school teacher and now teaches adults in a tertiary institution.

After gaining qualifications which have enabled her to teach psychology and personal development, Gloria has now begun on her new career. She expresses antipathy towards having to use the social security system after being financially self-sufficient. However, because of her husband's disability, the family income has been cut considerably and their lifestyle accordingly. Her job is, at present, giving her little satisfaction, but she hopes to improve her working conditions as her considerable skills become apparent and she becomes more confident.

Gloria has an arthritic condition which, while it does not inhibit her from physical activity, does give her 'bad days'; she has noticed that it fluctuates in response to stress. She is an optimistic and outgoing person, tending to shrug off her lot in life as the deal she has been handed, but she is now questioning the wisdom of that attitude. Her cream-cake dream explored earlier (p. 97), came at the end of a transit cycle and was the finale to the entire sequence, at which time Pluto had been out of orb, but had turned retrograde. Three days after her cream-cake dream, Pluto again turned direct and the entire Pluto-opposition-Sun phase ended. It is interesting, knowing the cream-cake dream, to examine the dream that occurred at the beginning of the period, when her difficulties were beginning to manifest. This dream Gloria called her 'kitchen dream'. Gloria's natal chart is repeated here for convenience.

Gloria recounted her dream: 'I had prepared a meal for my husband's friends and my parents. The friends brought along another elderly couple and said they knew I wouldn't mind as I always had plenty of food. The man said he had arranged a singer to entertain me while I cooked. The singer was one of my students but she didn't recognize me. Everyone but me was wearing party clothes. The girl sang and then demanded a fee. I didn't have any money so my mother paid and left with my father. John [husband] and his friends went into the sitting-room with a bottle of wine. A woman approached me at the stove and said the other old lady had invited some more of her friends as they had heard I always had plenty of food. A lot of people arrived including children who were very disruptive. The women sat around chatting and then went outside to where the men were congregated. I became very angry and demanded that John help me cook. He simply walked away. Women were complaining their children were hungry so I gave the children biscuits and cake, and the mothers all complained loudly. I then gave them cheese but it went mouldy in their hands. The women complained about the fruit trees and the drains so I told them to discuss it with John. They demanded that I fetch him. I did and when I got back to the kitchen all the food was congealed. I announced the dinner was served and the women all said it was disgusting and that I was very disorganized. The door opened and one of my friends came in and I was so pleased to see her but couldn't speak. Her husband looked around and said, "You've let them do it to you again." I hung my head in shame and began to cry; then I woke up.'

The similarity of the theme of this dream with that of the cream-cake dream is apparent and illustrates the non-linear nature of time in dreaming. In this dream the Moon is in the eleventh house and is connected by a square to Pluto in the ninth, highlighting the tension felt at a deep emotional level and the frustration Gloria feels at not being able to explore her own capacity to grow at a professional and intellectual level. The Moon also opposes Chiron on the cusp of the fifth and sixth houses, focusing clearly on Gloria's feelings of alienation and her desire to find her place within society, as well as focusing on health matters.

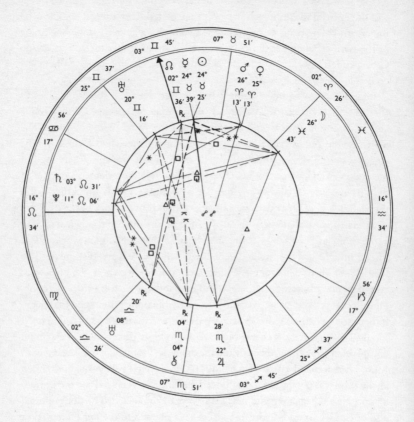

15. Gloria's Natal Chart

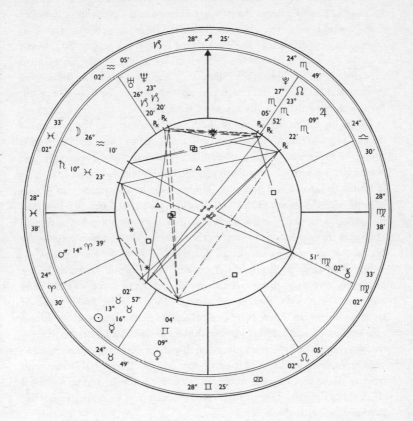

16. Gloria's Kitchen Dream (illustrating outer planet synastry)

As discussed, the eleventh house is where one might seek to find like souls, to be part of a family that is one of accord or collective kinship rather than genetic bonds. The eleventh house is where the self might seek to express being individual in a framework of compatible people. So Gloria's sense of being on the outside of society in some way, of not fitting in to expected norms, is highlighted. She is in a transition phase as she returns to work and finds a different social group, with whom she does not yet fit, for she changed the focus of her work applications.

Gloria, by the nature of her outer planets' transits is in the process of finding a new identity; the old must make way for the new and she begins a phase of finding where her new identity lies. Mercury, in the second house, is conjunct the Sun, opposes Pluto and the north node and Jupiter. It is also in a trine to Uranus and Neptune. The message in this dream puts Gloria in touch with the gestalt fields of all the outer planets and her own potential to transcend the traditions and safety zone of convention. A challenge is implied in the oppositions to Jupiter, the node and Pluto, which emphasizes her present ego state and its future potential.

Both these planets speak of her capacity to push out the limits of her safe boundaries to reach for and make sweeping changes to her lifestyle and sense of 'I'. She may, then, as symbolized by the node, find a sense of vocation in her life. There is wonderful insight in the dream, as the Moon opposes Chiron and Mercury opposes Jupiter. Both these planets have inner wisdom embedded in their meaning, but this might not have been recognized or fully amplified in Gloria's life up to now. Mercury's trine to Neptune and Uranus in the tenth house resonates with the potential for professional change, but indicates lack of form and structure and insecurity in her life outside the domestic sphere.

There is a calling, a voice from beyond the boundaries telling Gloria to find prestige through her professional standing, to find a new identity by exploring her own potential for academic and social growth and hence a new identity. The images are clear and representative of the whole situation: the safe life that she experiences in looking after people in an emotional and nurturing capacity in the domestic sphere must now be extended beyond the boundaries of the kitchen to students. The children in the dream, representing those she nurtures in domestic life, no longer give pleasure, indeed she seems to have little to offer them. The Moon in air illuminates her rational mind and separates her from the emotional dependence of being needed.

Synastry indicates the incoming nature of outer planets' transits as the aspects are applying and inner planets show the Moon square Sun, Mercury and Jupiter. Resolution will not be easy, as Gloria identifies strongly with the second house of material comfort. Her natal Sun and Mercury are predisposed in such a way that she identifies herself with Taurean matters of stability and solid and reliable comfort gained through material manifestation. Being reliable gives her a sense of identity and this synastry is interesting as the dream chart Sun/Mercury opposition Jupiter is a repeat of her natal propensity. Jupiter is retrograde in both charts; the potential for growth occurs at an inner level and is accomplished through quiet achievement. Approval, being loved by those whom she nurtures and for whom she provides security, is important to Gloria yet it frustrates and wounds her sense of well-being. Mars in the dream chart does not have much strength. Apart from a sextile to Venus, it strikes something of a silent note, and is not involved in aspects with the Moon or Mercury. In synastry Mars is novile natal Sun and Mercury, implying that intuitive action will enable her to reach her ideal and gain vocational satisfaction, but there is little motivation beyond making Gloria aware of her need to seek her true identity.

It is unlikely, then, that this dream will do anything more than alert Gloria and she may think about its implications but take little action. Overall, the dream seems to be one of awareness rather than action; it sows seeds in Gloria's mind enabling her to hear the message, and the message was to be repeated later. In dialogue she understood the dream intent clearly, and began to take steps towards adjusting to her new lifestyle. She began to document her dreams from that point.

The images of Gloria's kitchen dream and her cream-cake dream evoke similar dramas and both dreams in some way deal with Gloria's search for a new identity consistent with the kind of experience which comes when Pluto and the Sun are in such a challenging aspect. This aspect coincides with other outer planet transits which also suggest change at a psychic level. The chronology of these dreams is irrelevant, in that both dreams address different facets of Gloria's renaissance.

The cream cake dream helps in reconciling the unfamiliar stage that has come about in her marriage as she and John reverse the socially accepted roles. The kitchen dream leads Gloria to review her professional and group affiliations and encourages her to seek a fresh place and new associations which can give her a sense of belonging to a collective environment which lies beyond her normal, conditioned expectations.

	☽	☉	☿	♀	♂	♃	♄	♅	♆	♇	⚷	☊	As	Mc
☽		□ 1S44	□ 1S30	✶ 0S56	✶ 0A02	□ 3S41								
☉									□ 1S56				□ 3A31	
☿													□ 0S22	
♀							△ 0S44		✶ 2A01					
♂		N 0S14	N 0A00						△ 3S33				△ 1A55	
♃									□ 1S43					
♄									⊼ 0A42					
♅	✶ 0S22	△ 1A55	△ 1A41	□ 1A07	□ 0A07									
♆		△ 1S04	△ 1S19	□ 1S53	□ 2S52	✶ 0A51								
♇	△ 0A21	☍ 2A39	☍ 2A25	⊼ 1A51	⊼ 0A52									
⚷										✶ 1A12	□ 0S15			□ 0A53
☊	△ 2S50	☍ 0S32	☍ 0S47	⊼ 1S21	☌ 1A23									
As	☌ 1A55								⊼ 2A32				⊼ 2A55	
Mc	□ 1A42		△ 3A12	△ 2A12					⊼ 2A19					

17. Gloria's Kitchen Dream (down) to Gloria's Natal Chart (across)

Over the entire phase, which lasted for three years, Gloria dreamed many dreams, all of which forced her to re-examine her attitudes, her emotions, her thinking and her role in life as it began to be destroyed and then rebuilt. Many dream experiences were arduous, as she faced facets of her own personality and emotions that were not easy to comprehend, and many dreams were of nightmarish proportions, but each healed and gave Gloria the opportunity to bring repressed and stifled feelings to the surface for reconciliation. Imprisoned rage and impotence were dealt with by recognizing them and actively doing something to release them in a managed and non-destructive way.

It can be seen in the cream-cake dream that Pluto in the final retrograde stage backtracks, giving Gloria a last reminder of the way things used to be and the progress she has made. There is no way to be definitive about this, but the images of that dream, of a funeral, a final goodbye to old patterns, and Gloria's supportive 'other self' in the guise of a friend, are reassuring. At the time of writing Gloria is revelling in the transit of Uranus in opposition to her natal Saturn. She feels free of the constraints of guilt and her relationship with John is a mutually delightful exploration of their own latent gifts.

Gloria works hard on allowing others to do things for her and it is several months since I heard the word 'martyr'! Her professional life has burgeoned and she is thinking of opening a private counselling practice. She listens to the messages of her dreams as an essential part of the process of actively and consciously reworking her life, and will no doubt be able to help others work through their dreams. The wheel has turned – what was a critical phase has passed and her life has become creative and productive. She will no doubt have other difficult phases to deal with, but she now has the power to approach such phases with less foreboding, knowing that the unconscious helps to solve and resolve, prompt and heal.

DIALOGUE WITH THE DREAMER

The relationship between dreamworker and client, individual and dream is a sensitive one, in which an exchange takes place that promotes healing. The dreamworker, by dialoguing with the dreamer's inner life, in effect enters the landscape of the dreamer's soul. One needs to be sure not to trespass on this sacred soil but instead to plant seeds that will grow and enrich the dreamer's psychic life. One must remember that the meaning of the dream is subjective to the dreamer's experience. Dreams reflect life. Linear time, or ego-centred time, is inconstant. The day before the dream had no meaning to soul, but once life is dreamed, the substance of the dream remains as a constant truth in the reality of soul. The dream reflects that inner truth and derives its meaning through subjective connections – hence all dreams have meaning.

So, while symbols may have both a collective and archetypal meaning, they must always have a link to the dreamer's inner reality. Without this personal and individual connection, dreams can mean nothing to the dreamer, the dream acquires reality and exists because the dreamer makes a connection; in effect, a symbol can only be meaningful in the dream image if it is recognized.

Dreams can be very confusing and often seem to make little sense when we try to find a connection with the dreamer's day-to-day life. The unconscious tends to create dreams which carry components not only of subjective experiences but also those of the collective and of the dreamer's past and future. Some of the symbols might be difficult for the dreamer to identify because they come from the storehouse of the collective and the emotive reaches of the dreamer's soul.

The dreamworker plays an active role but also, more importantly, a mediating role in helping a client to understand the collective language of a dream and not imposing his or her own personal meaning. Only in this way can he participate in this sacred process. By setting aside personal ego considerations, interpretations of his own dreams or dreams related to him by other dreamers, no matter how similar they may be to those of the client, he is able to act in the capacity of guide. The attempt to mediate the dream is not the dreamworker's journey, and arbitrary or personal interpretation will not help the dreamer to resolve whatever is surfacing in the dream.

It is essential to have a basic understanding of symbolism. Dialogue is achieved through interpretation and controlled amplification of the dream, by using the context of the dream as a framework and the planetary transits to gain an overall perspective. Dreams that lead to a meaningful conclusion from which the dreamer gains knowledge enables a compensatory transformation to occur. This transformation occurs as the dreamer is guided into a personal understanding of the unconscious language of the dream. The capacity to do so is embedded in the dreamer's nature and is stimulated into consciousness through dialogue with the dreamworker. Studying what a symbol may mean in a collective sense enriches not only the astrologer's personal life but his professional life as well. Through such study the astrologer or dreamworker gains tools for fruitful dialogue and enhanced understanding of symbolic life. This is the greatest reward. Responsible dreamworkers or astrological practitioners are those who know their own limitations and are aware that they need to be alert to the possibility that those with whom they work may need referral to other therapists; astrology cannot give all the answers, nor can dreamwork alone.

We see, then, that conditions apply in interpreting and understanding dreams. These conditions centre on the context of the dream and are described by the natal chart, current transits, life situation of the dreamer and most specifically by the dream chart and its synastry. To amplify the dream is to take the images, explore them within this context and come to an understanding of its personal implications. It is very tempting when faced with a dream filled with archetypal symbols to expand too much, to inflate rather than amplify. The dreamworker must not force or cajole, but should escort the dreamer through the dream, acting in a Mercurial way to guide without judgement. Even though one might see a deeper interpretation than that discovered by the dreamer, or a different one, the dream belongs to the dreamer and the fact that their subjective interpretation is ultimately the most meaningful must be respected.

Mercurial tools are words, ideas, abstractions and the capacity to think laterally. Mercury manifests through such instruments as paper and pencils, art materials, tape-recorders, books, pictures, conversation and dialogue, all of which may help to explore the inner world. A valuable method of exploring a dream is drawing the dream. This can be useful when working with children, or when the dream indicates a connectedness with childhood experiences. Surprising imagery is revealed when the images are graphically re-created; figures and symbols that were not apparent in the telling of the dream magically appear in pictorial form.

There are two main ways in which one can work with the astrology of dreaming. The first is with the regular client who is experiencing a growth phase or particular outward manifestations of transits, and desires to understand their psychodynamics. Dreamwork can be an immensely valuable tool for monitoring progress and is possibly the most satisfying side of the work, as one can see a client gain authority over his own life and become his own mentor. The second is the casual client who is simply perturbed by a dream. This is no less satisfying if one can be instrumental in leading such a person to examine their own inner life. The dream chart alone, without the natal synastry, can be very effective in such a case. (Of course the astrologer can gain an idea of the likely transits, just by inquiring the age of the client!)

While we each have our own way of working with a client, I find it useful to explain the dream chart and the Moon's house meaning before even hearing the dream. In this way, we establish a context that defines but does not confine the exploration of the dream. Amplification is then possible, without the dream imagery masking the intent of the dream. This gives an unconfirming but controlled context in which to journey towards understanding and can be explained to the dreamer without using technical astrological terms. Once an understanding of the context of the dream is established, exploration can begin. A useful way to do this is by drawing a circle in which the key words of the dream are placed. This becomes a mandala which is the matrix from which each word and image, and their associations, both metaphorical and personal, can be explored and amplified until the dreamer makes sense of them.

It is the role of the astrologer to guide the dreamer to a point where each symbol makes some personal sense. Many symbols may not be immediately personally identified by the dreamer, or may be found confusing. These are the symbols to which the astrologer might apply what I call an 'archetypal value'. That is, to suggest something from the collective root meaning of such a symbol and then allow the dreamer to explore it further. For example, numbers often come up in dreams. They may have little personal meaning to a dreamer beyond the pragmatic meaning – balancing a cheque-book, keeping time, etc., all left-brain activities – but the non-rational and imaginal right-brain function applies to them as well, only here the meaning is rather more comprehensive.

Numbers have a significance in dreams which goes beyond their mundane numeric values. They have a meaning rooted in the cosmic order of the universe, of humankind, and the structure of society – a meaning embedded in the collective unconscious. Numbers can express in quite a precise way something that leads back to the beginnings of time and universal order, as any numerologist will confirm. Tom Chetwyn says, '. . . the symbolism of numbers has since become so abstracted from what roots it may have had, and so complex, that it seems to have become more of a construction by the conscious mind. So it has lost much of its immediate impact. The symbolism is more consistent (and interesting) where the links are still obvious with other aspects of symbolism. For example, seven is related to the planets (or Great Bear) and therefore the celestial sphere, and twelve to the zodiac and the Olympian Gods.'[1] He explores numbers further, saying of the number four – which frequently occurs in dreams – 'Four. Completion, actuality in the realm of matter, with its many fourfold aspects: see Directions; Elements; Seasons.'[2]

By exploring those symbols which we associate with numbers, the dreamworker can understand the themes which relate to the material realities of a person's life. For instance through the number four and the dream of 'standing at a crossroads' one can infer that the dreamer is at a point of material choice, or change of direction, in the matter shown by the dream chart. Often, crossroads dreams will divide into two or three distinct scenarios – for instance, the dreamer might find himself first at a crossroads, then in a town, then at home, then in a forest. Quite often the fourth direction, the one not featured in the dream, is the unfamiliar territory worthy of consideration. This brings the dreamer to a point in his life that is nearing completion. If all four directions are features of the dream, the crossroads and its related number four implies that a cycle is completed and a new one about to begin. It is worth recalling that the Greek god Hermes (Mercury) is the god of crossroads!

The cyclic nature of the dreamer's life is confirmed by the dream chart and its synastry, and by the outer planetary transits. It is common for a symbol to become distanced from its roots as language changes and evolves, and many symbols lose their impact in the conscious, ego-oriented life. The astrologer could suggest a root archetypal value for a symbol within the context of the dream, and thus guide the dreamer through explaining and offering suggestions, in their exploration into the personal connection. In this way the objective and the subjective intertwine in dialogue. Tracing the clues by connecting the amplified images will eventually result in the dream message being understood. Dialogue means to use *two* minds to understand the dream, yet the meaning belongs only to one. The astrologer suggests, guides and, by keeping the dream in context, structures the direction of the dreamer's interpretation. Left-brain and right-brain activity interface and complement both participants. Motifs expressed in the dream are thus enriched and filled out to give more depth and breadth of meaning. An example is a dialogue with Charlotte, a career woman in her late fifties.

Charlotte dreamed the following dream: 'I was at home and my husband and daughter came and cut off my hands. They put the hands into a bucket

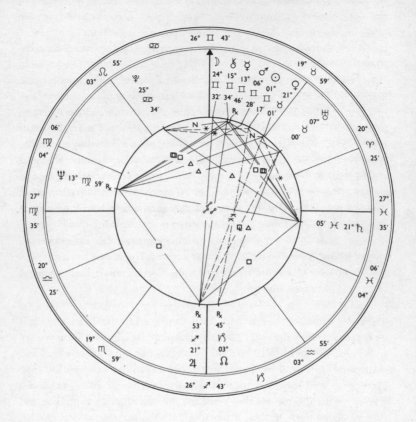

18. Charlotte's Natal Chart

of water and scrubbed them clean then stuck them back on to my wrists. I felt no pain and the blood didn't worry me, but I woke up feeling a bit angry.'

Charlotte had worked as an executive secretary for a multinational company for twenty-five years. She has been separated from her husband, but has recently been reunited with him, and they have bought a new home together. Her spiritual explorations were the source of many disputes and, together with a large age difference (he being some twenty years older than she), had contributed to the breakdown of her marriage. However, she had found that when living separately, they remained good friends and, eventually, because of his ageing, she had decided to return to the marriage.

At work there had been an industrial strike that had reached extreme and violent proportions. She admits to a secret sympathy with the workers but was torn by her political role as an executive. She had worked for the same man for all of her twenty-five years, but after the dispute he was replaced by a younger, more confrontational man with whom she feels little empathy. She is concerned at how she might function in the new management situation and is trying to find a way to adjust to the changes and fit in to the new regime. Well aware of her own abilities, she understands the politics of paying lip service, but until now she has loved her job and devoted herself heart and soul to it; now she feels she must view it less as a vocation and more as a means of earning a living. This causes her some discomfort.

This is a third-house dream, the area of communication, of education, environment and learned skills. This house also connects to ethics and morals that have been taught and which are well established in the psyche – ethics and morals that may not have been questioned in the past. Charlotte now questions the truths in her life and is struggling to establish her own morality – the ethics instilled in childhood, and which have stood her in good stead until now, are in conflict with those prevailing in the environment. Legal, social and environmental matters have come into focus.

The Moon in earth implies the static and predictable way in which she is thinking and implies that such thinking is habitual and well ingrained, and has been a sound footing on which to base her life and develop her practical skills. It shows the realities of her environment and indicates that she might be frustrated in wanting to express something that convention inhibits. There is a profound truth in the apparent brevity and simplicity of the dream, as so often happens with third-house dreams – simplicity masks complexity.

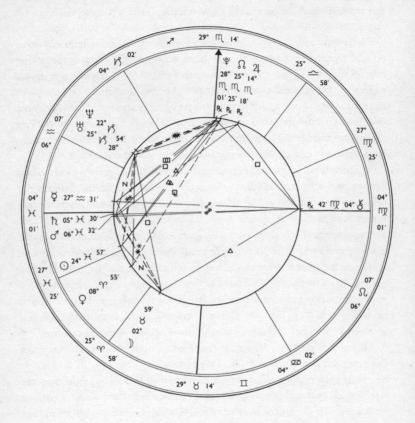

19. Charlotte's Hands-off Dream (illustrating dream dialogue)

The moon draws Uranus in the eleventh house into the picture, expressing the tension she is experiencing in connection with group ideologies and ideals and collective values, her sense of kinship with the wider family and her incapacity to express that tension. (She is a sympathizer with the common man.) The changes that have occurred in her work environment do not sit comfortably for Charlotte but she is unsure of how to express her opinions or dissatisfaction freely.

Her belonging is no longer the same as it was, as many co-workers have lost their jobs and there is no longer a sense of family in the workforce. The Moon also forms a trine aspect with Chiron in the seventh house, so healing is available through the dream, regardless of its bloody imagery. It highlights Charlotte's capacity to heal herself and others, rooted in her unconscious. The Moon draws attention to the prophetic and sagacious side of her personality so that she will be able to gain great insight from it after a period of introspection.

Mercury squares retrograde Pluto and the node in the ninth. Mercury's message is about profound change, healing through catharsis, but a catharsis accompanied by tension and some pain. She is at odds with her past sense of vocation and through the pressure of this aspect may find the message is that she is not so committed to her career as she used to be and needs to find a different path. Mercury's twelfth-house position states that the demon must be confronted and, out of the turmoil of hurt and anguish, new life can emerge. Charlotte needs to examine whether she is indeed capable of paying lip service.

It is interesting here to pause and consider the north node, which brings associations with people into play, and the conjunction with Pluto, which has manifested in Charlotte's new boss – the 'hatchet man' – whom she has coincidentally dubbed 'little Pluto'. The opposition to Chiron brings potential for healing in relationships and clearly implies that there is a breach, a wound that the Chiron part of her personality can bridge.

Examination of the synastry grid shows the outer planet's phase of Pluto opposing her natal Sun. This is outside the limit of natal transits work but, with Pluto retrograde, indicates that once it turns direct, it will close the orb at the end of the year. The dream occurred in March 1994 and in January 1995 Pluto entered Sagittarius and turned retrograde within days – a brief foretaste of things to come. It was not to come within the one-degree orb of opposition until later but, as can be seen, by using a wider orb in

	☽	☉	☿	♀	♂	♃	♄	♅	♆	♇	⚷	☊	As	Mc
☽	0A07		N 0A46									△ 0A46		
☉	□ 0S24					□ 3S03	☌ 3S51			△ 0A36			☍ 2A38	□ 1A46
☿	△ 2S58	□ 3A45								⊼ 1S57			⊼ 0A03	△ 0S48
♀		0A55			✶ 2S27									
♂					□ 0S04				✶ 0A27			✶ 2S47		
♃		⊼ 0A31						✶ 0A18			⊼ 1S16			□ 2A34
♄					□ 0A58			✶ 1A29				✶ 1S44		
♅	⊼ 0S55									☍ 0A05			△ 2A06	⊼ 1A15
♆	⊼ 1A38			△ 1S52	⚼ 1S26		✶ 1S48			☍ 2A39				
♇		☍ 3S15								△ 2A26			✶ 0A25	⊼ 1A17
⚷		□ 3A25			□ 1S45		△ 2S17			N 0S51		△ 0A57		
☊	⊼ 0A52									△ 0S08			✶ 2S09	⊼ 1S18
As		□ 2A43			□ 2A27		✶ 2A58					✶ 0A15		
Mc		☍ 2A02								△ 3A40			✶ 1A39	

20. Charlotte's Hands-off Dream (down) to Charlotte's Natal Chart (across)

dreamwork, we are able to anticipate or even pre-empt this phase of potential major renaissance.

The unconscious does exactly that, but consciousness impedes us from hearing the message. At the time of the dream, Pluto is in trine to its own natal position. The potential difficulties may well be avoided if some constructive changes are made so that, by the time Pluto comes into a closer orb, the changes can be more fruitful. Neptune is in trine to Venus, so Charlotte's personal values, affections and loyalties are infused with idealism and perhaps romantic illusion. Her reunion with her marriage partner may be as a result of her sympathetic and idealistic nature rather than of practical consideration. Uranus and Neptune are in opposition to natal Pluto, and her experiences might be such that illusion is shattered. This aspect stimulates her tenth-house Pluto and its association with power in the workplace and authority over herself and others, and might effectively be the subliminal reason for her feeling undermined in her profession – challenges in outer conditions reflect the inner spiritual challenge, concomitant with an awakening awareness of something outside the material world. The implication here is that she needs to examine just what such power entails at a subjective level and what price she might pay spiritually and morally by paying lip service. Uranus is exact in opposition to natal Pluto, so might be seen as a pivotal or central point in outer planet transits and the dream may be one of great significance as a crisis of consciousness occurs.

There are conflicting energies at play, as the challenging oppositions and the harmonious trines both contact her Sun, Venus and Pluto. This is a time of promising change for Charlotte. In discussing the dream, we began by placing all the symbol keywords in a central mandala and then explored each symbol through dialogue, keeping it within the context of the dream. This concluded with the writing of each motif – effectively 'naming' it and bringing it into conscious context. Where Charlotte was unable to make a connection, 'archetypal values' were suggested, and then explored further. Each central keyword was explored, and the amplification sheet is reproduced here as illustration. Motifs contained in a broken circle are those that were suggested to Charlotte.

Charlotte left our consultation to rethink her relationship to the new situation at her workplace and to examine her personal ethics. Because she can adopt a professional as well as a caring attitude, we had discussed the need to try and see how difficult it must be for her new boss to come into a difficult situation and play the role of 'little Pluto'. She intended to think

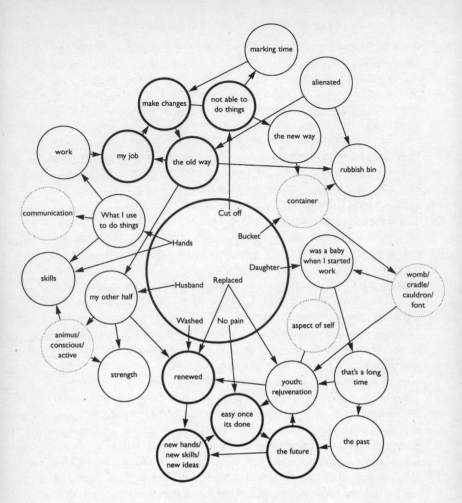

21. Dialogue Mandala

The dream highlights areas of ethical, religious and moral values, communication, unspoken words, learned skills and the environment. It involves a connection with peers with whom there is a sense of 'belonging'. There is a message here about reconciling differences, about exchange in equal proportions and whether personal values and ethics fit with those in the environment. There is some tension, as it seems to warn of impending upheaval that could be unpleasant, but which would eventuate as a major turning point in life. Vocational, personal, intellectual, moral and ethical growth is the main thrust of the dream.

about whether it was feasible for her to attempt to strike a balance between the old ways and the new, and whether she needed to make a distinct choice between the hierarchical structures and her own ideology. We discussed the connotations of the forthcoming Pluto opposition to her Sun, both in its positive and negative potentials. In essence, her thoughts were to be centred not so much on what she should do, but on whether she could be ethically creative, make adjustments and transform lip service into commitment. She needed to decide whether her personal morality was perhaps no longer viable now that previous management methods had given way to a cut-and-thrust system: 'outside' contractors replacing whole families of workers; retrenchments and fiscal packages representing people as commodities; profit coming before personal allegiance.

I was not surprised when Charlotte telephoned me later the same day and said that she had had the task of processing redundancy notices to hundreds of employees, many of whom she had known for many years. 'Little Pluto' had made the decisions and she was to be the messenger. She said she had looked at her hands while typing the letters and they seemed not to be her hands. As she looked at them, they seemed to speak to her, saying, 'We are clean – we should not be doing this work!' She had decided to resign. I suggested that she spend some time thinking about her decision, and then approach 'little Pluto' and discuss her moral dilemma.

Several days later she telephoned to say that, to her surprise, he had been very understanding of her situation and had asked her to stay for the rest of the year while he himself was settling in. Her Neptune and Venus transits came into focus in a positive and realistic way and she did stay for the rest of the year. While the new management methods were still alien to her, she did manage to establish a reasonable relationship with her boss.

In January 1995, as Pluto made a brief sortie into Sagittarius and came within orb of opposing her natal Sun, she left her employment with a very satisfactory golden handshake. Some months later, she phoned for an appointment to discuss whether she and her husband would again be better living separate lives. She recalled the significance of the hands-off dream and was convinced that she had not completely manifested its meaning. She told me she had dreamed during the night but did not remember the time. In the dream, a golden man appeared and said, 'I am Apollo.' She asked me, 'Who is Apollo?' I said I would tell her Apollo's story when she arrived. She arrived late, eager to tell me what had happened on the way to my office. She had taken a wrong turn and ended up in the dockland area, where she saw a ship loading base metal ore, and was amazed to see that the name of the ship was *Apollo*.

Our consultation began with a discussion about what she had been doing in her retirement – while she enjoyed her freedom, she did find domestic life a bit tedious and said that every time she got a bucket out to do anything domestic, she remembered the dream and her talking hands. The relationship with her husband was insufferable for both. She mentioned the hands-off dream as a significant turning-point in her life, and I reminded her that the dream had indicated a beginning as well as an ending.

I related the myth of Apollo, the sun god, and we explored the idea of Pluto opposing the Sun and whether there might be a message in the symbol that manifested in her dream of Apollo. Charlotte was fascinated by the symbol of the ship, loading material that symbolizes Pluto's 'underground' connections. We talked about the transformation she was experiencing from her business, ego-oriented life to a more inner symbolic life, confirmed by her recognition of symbols in her daily life. She telephoned again a few days later to tell me that, to her amazement, on her return, she had again driven by the docklands and found a place where yachts were berthed. This time she had seen a yacht named *Apollo*! I was not to hear from Charlotte for some weeks; then she phoned one day to say she had separated again from her husband, amicably, and to the relief of both of them. She had bought an airline ticket and was 'leaving her third house for her ninth and maybe to find Apollo'. She is now exploring a different landscape.

Notes

1. Mapping the Dream Landscape

1. Dr Peter O'Connor, *Dreams and the Search for Meaning*, Methuen Haynes, Australia, 1986, p. 5.
2. Dr C. G. Jung, *Memories, Dreams, Reflections*, Harper Collins (Flamingo), London, 1983, p. 413.
3. ibid., p. 221.
4. Jolande Jacobi, *The Psychology of C. G. Jung*, citing Jung, English edn, Yale University Press, 1973, p. 73.

2. Mercury – Guide to the Dream Journey

1. Jacobi, ibid., p. 97.
2. ibid., p. 97.
3. Graham Dunstan Martin, *Shadows in the Cave*, Penguin Books (Arkana), London, 1990, p. 19.
4. Jung, op. cit., p. 68.
5. ibid., p. 414.

3. Moon – Illuminating Soul's Intent

1. Dane Rudhyar, *The Lunation Cycle*, Aurora Press, Santa Fe, USA, 1967.
2. ibid., p. 43.

4. The Inner Planets – Meeting Facets of Self

1. Katharine Merlin, *Character and Fate*, Penguin Books (Arkana), London, p. 14.
2. Bruno Huber, *Astrological Psychosynthesis*, Aquarian Press, HarperCollins, London, 1991, p. 49.
3. Howard Sasportas, *The Twelve Houses*, Aquarian Press, HarperCollins, London, 1985, p. 229.

4. Erin Sullivan, *Saturn in Transit: Boundaries of Mind, Body and Soul*, Penguin Books (Arkana), London, 1991.

5. Transpersonal Planets – Beyond the Threshold

1. Liz Greene, *The Astrology of Fate*, Sam Weiser Inc., York Beach, Maine, 1984, p. 117.
2. ibid., p. 47.
3. ibid., p. 50.
4. ibid., p. 47.
5. Sasportas, op. cit., p. 18.
6. Melanie Reinhart, *Chiron and the Healing Journey*, Penguin Books (Arkana), London, 1989.
7. Ken Wilbur, *Up from Eden*, Routledge & Kegan Paul, London, 1983.
8. ibid., p. 45.
9. ibid., p. 213.
10. ibid., p. 325.
11. ibid., pp. 12–14, 330.

6. Houses – Mandala of Self

1. Jacobi, op. cit., citing Jung, p. 27.
2. ibid., citing Jung, p. 27.
3. ibid., p. 28.
4. Sasportas, op. cit., p. 43.
5. ibid., p. 61.

7. Aspects – Synthesis of Self

1. Erin Sullivan, *Retrograde Planets: Traversing the Inner Landscape*, Penguin Books (Arkana), London, 1992.
2. Robert Hand, *Planets in Transit*, Whitford Press, Schiffer Publishing, USA, 1976.

8. Dream Astrology – Towards Wholeness

1. Tom Chetwyn, *A Dictionary of Symbols*, Collins Publishing Group (Paladin), London, 1982, p. 281.
2. ibid., p. 286.

Index

Figures in italics refer to illustrations

PENGUIN

ARKANA

NEW AGE BOOKS FOR MIND, BODY & SPIRIT

With over 200 titles currently in print, Arkana is the leading name in quality books for mind, body and spirit. Arkana encompasses the spirituality of both East and West, ancient and new. A vast range of interests is covered, including Psychology and Transformation, Health, Science and Mysticism, Women's Spirituality, Zen, Western Traditions and Astrology.

If you would like a catalogue of Arkana books, please write to:

Sales Department – Arkana
Penguin Books USA Inc.
375 Hudson Street
New York, NY 10014

Arkana Marketing Department
Penguin Books Ltd
27 Wrights Lane
London W8 5TZ

Available while stocks last.

PENGUIN

ARKANA

NEW AGE BOOKS FOR MIND, BODY & SPIRIT

A SELECTION OF TITLES

The Revised Waite's Compendium of Natal Astrology
Alan Candlish

This completely revised edition retains the basic structure of Waite's classic work while making major improvements to accuracy and readability. With a new computer-generated Ephemeris, complete for the years 1900 to 2010, and a Table of Houses that now allows astrologers to choose between seven house systems, it provides all the information on houses, signs and planets the astrologer needs to draw up and interpret a full natal chart.

A Time to Heal   Beata Bishop

The inspiring story of a woman's triumph over life-threatening disease – through an unorthodox therapy. When Beata Bishop's cancer spread into the lymphatic system, she rejected the options of surgery or 'wait-to-die' and travelled to the Gerson clinic in Mexico, for therapy based on optimum nutrition and thorough detoxification. Over a decade later, she is fit and well, enjoying life to the full.

Tao Te Ching   The Richard Wilhelm Edition

Encompassing philosophical speculation and mystical reflection, the *Tao Te Ching* has been translated more often than any other book except the Bible, and more analysed than any other Chinese classic. Richard Wilhelm's acclaimed 1910 translation is here made available in English.

The Book of the Dead   E. A. Wallis Budge

Intended to give the deceased immortality, the Ancient Egyptian *Book of the Dead* was a vital piece of 'luggage' on the soul's journey to the other world, providing for every need: victory over enemies, the procurement of friendship and – ultimately – entry into the kingdom of Osiris.

Astrology: A Key to Personality   Jeff Mayo

Astrology: A Key to Personality is designed to help you find out who you *really* are. A book for beginners wanting simple instructions on how to interpret a chart, as well as for old hands seeking fresh perspectives, it offers a unique system of self-discovery.

PENGUIN

ARKANA

NEW AGE BOOKS FOR MIND, BODY & SPIRIT

A SELECTION OF TITLES

Light on Life Hart deFouw and Robert Svoboda

Jyotish or Indian astrology is an ancient and complex method of exploring the nature of time and space and its effect upon the individual. Formerly a closed book to the West, the subject has now been clarified and explained by Hart deFouw and Robert Svoboda, two experts and long-term practitioners.

The Moment of Astrology Geoffrey Cornelius

'This is an extraordinary book ... I believe that within the astrological tradition it is the most important since the great flowering of European astrology more than three hundred years ago ... Quietly but deeply subversive, this is a book for lovers of wisdom' – from the Foreword by Patrick Curry

Homage to the Sun: The Wisdom of the Magus of Strovolos
Kyriacos C. Markides

Homage to the Sun continues the adventure into the mysterious and extraordinary world of the spiritual teacher and healer Daskalos, the 'Magus of Strovolos'. The logical foundations of Daskalos's world of other dimensions are revealed to us – invisible masters, past-life memories and guardian angels, all explained by the Magus with great lucidity and scientific precision.

The Eagle's Gift Carlos Castaneda

In the sixth book in his astounding journey into sorcery, Castaneda returns to Mexico. Entering once more a world of unknown terrors, hallucinatory visions and dazzling insights, he discovers that he is to replace the Yaqui Indian don Juan as leader of the apprentice sorcerers – and learns of the significance of the Eagle.

PENGUIN

ARKANA

NEW AGE BOOKS FOR MIND, BODY & SPIRIT

A SELECTION OF TITLES

Daimonic Reality Patrick Harpur

Mysterious lights in the sky, phantom animals, visions of the Virgin Mary, UFOs, fairies, alien abductions ... Such anomalies have appeared throughout the centuries and, despite the denials of Church and Science, continue to be reported all over the world. 'A startling "field guide to the Otherworld" which should stop even the sceptical in their tracks' – *Observer*. 'A brave, thought-provoking book' – *Daily Mail*

The Second Ring of Power Carlos Castaneda

Carlos Castaneda's journey into the world of sorcery has captivated millions. In this fifth book, he introduces the reader to Dona Soledad, whose mission is to test Castaneda by a series of terrifying tricks. Thus Castaneda is initiated into experiences so intense, so profoundly disturbing, as to be an assault on reason and on every preconceived notion of life ...

Dialogues with Scientists and Sages: The Search for Unity
Renée Weber

In their own words, contemporary scientists and mystics – from the Dalai Lama to Stephen Hawking – share with us their richly diverse views on space, time, matter, energy, life, consciousness, creation and our place in the scheme of things. Through the immediacy of verbatim dialogue, we encounter scientists who endorse mysticism, and those who oppose it; mystics who dismiss science, and those who embrace it.

Women in Search of the Sacred Anne Bancroft

This fascinating book surveys the careers of ten very different women and examines the ways in which they have developed their spiritual lives. Some, for example writer Susan Howatch, find that serving God is the key to a spiritually fulfilling life, whereas for Danah Zohar, a convert to Judaism, the sacred mystery of existence is allied to quantum physics.

PENGUIN

ARKANA

NEW AGE BOOKS FOR MIND, BODY & SPIRIT

CONTEMPORARY ASTROLOGY

Series Editor: Erin Sullivan

The ancient science of astrology, founded on the correlation between celestial movements and terrestrial events, recognizes the universe as an indivisible whole in which all parts are interconnected. Mirroring this perception of the unity of life, modern physics has revealed the web of relationships underlying everything in existence. Despite the inevitable backlash as old paradigms expire, we are now entering an age in which scientific explanations and models of the cosmos are in accord with basic astrological principles and beliefs. In such a climate, astrology is poised to emerge once again as a serious tool for a greater understanding of our true nature. In readable books written by experts, Arkana's Contemporary Astrology series offers all the insight and practical wisdom of the newest vanguard of astrological thought.

Titles already published or in preparation:

The Gods of Change: Pain, Crisis and the Transits of Uranus, Neptune and Pluto Howard Sasportas

Chiron and the Healing Journey: An Astrological and Psychological Perspective Melanie Reinhart

Working With Astrology Michael Harding and Charles Harvey

Saturn: A New Look at an Old Devil Liz Greene

The Karmic Journey Judy Hall

The God Between Freda Edis

Saturn in Transit Erin Sullivan

The Moment of Astrology Geoffrey Cornelius

Retrograde Planets: Traversing the Inner Landscape Erin Sullivan

Dynasty: The Astrology of Family Dynamics Erin Sullivan

A Handbook of Medical Astrology Jane Ridder-Patrick